I was an Olympic
Volunteer

– MIKE COOPER–

An environmentally friendly book printed and bound in England by
www.printondemand-worldwide.com

i

www.fast-print.net/store.php

I was an Olympic Volunteer
Copyright © Mike Cooper 2011

ISBN 978-178035-029-5

First published 2011 by
FASTPRINT PUBLISHING
Peterborough, England.

Thanks

I would life to thank those people who have helped me in the publishing of this book.

Katie Jarvis who has given me valuable editorial help and general guidance.

Athletes Dame Mary Peters, Roger Black and Richard Phelps in verifying quotes. Richard Hopkins of Devizes for advice about Judo.

The Atlanta Centenary Olympic Games organisers and IBM for giving me the opportunity to be a volunteer.

Angela, my wife, for her patience.

Half of the profits made from the sale of this book will be donated to the charity

END POLIO NOW

An international campaign of The Rotary Foundation

Could this be you?

In front of me ten thousand of the greatest athletes in the world had just marched into the stadium and were assembled in the centre of the running track. They were smiling and waving excitedly to their families, friends and supporters in the stands. In the block of seats behind, not far away, sat the President of the USA, Bill Clinton, the President of the Olympic Committee, Juan Antonio Samaranch and many heads of the great nations of the world. In the stands were eighty five thousand spectators who had paid top dollar for their tickets. At home over two billion people from all over the world would be watching the Opening Ceremony of the 1996 Centenary Olympic Games on their television sets. The Atlanta Olympic Stadium was packed to capacity and things were really buzzing. I could hardly believe it, I was actually there! Yes, these were the most exciting moments of my life.

A relay of runners had carried the torch through most of the states of the USA to the base of the cauldron where the Olympic flame would burn during the Games. As the last runner climbed the ramp, the scoreboard revealed the answer to the closely guarded secret of the name of the person honoured to light the Olympic Flame. It was 'Muhammed Ali'. A mighty roar went up from everyone in the stadium. With a hand shaking from Parkinson's Disease he struggled to light the fuse to the flame. Grown men had tears in their eyes. Seconds later the Olympic flame lit the summer sky.

The Centenary Olympic Games were under-way.

Atlanta Olympic Games 1996.

Preliminaries

'Would you like to be an Olympic volunteer?

I saw this advertisement in the company magazine, and my immediate reaction was " yes , what do I have to do?" I submitted my details to the authorities, and shortly afterwards a multi-page application form arrived in the post. It wanted to know just about everything there was to know about me, including names of referees, details of employment, state of health and past addresses.

I had recently retired from IBM, and was still on the mailing list for the company magazine. IBM also happened to be one of the ten major companies sponsoring the Atlanta Olympics, so providing references and verifying personal information was easy for me. A few weeks later I received a card which said "Congratulations, you have been selected to be a volunteer". My immediate reaction was that's wonderful, but what exactly do they want me to do?

I phoned the volunteer management number in Atlanta, and was told that I had been selected for 'stadium management'. It sounded a splendid title. I had visions of sitting in the command module surveying the stadium and master-minding all activities that went on below. Actually it wasn't quite like that, because he went on to say that it meant I would be an usher in the main athletics stadium. Nevertheless my reaction to this news was sheer joy. I would be working in the location which would be the hub of activity, where the opening and closing ceremonies took place, and all the finals of the track and field events would be contested. He asked if I was still interested? Yes, I certainly was, in fact metaphorically I nearly bit his hand off.

A training package was to follow, and I was asked if I could be available for two major athletics events in Atlanta in the weeks before the games. One of these was to be the trials where the USA team would be selected. It would have been a great event to see, but it was a month or so before the games.

I pointed out that this would mean another expensive transatlantic flight, so he told me not to worry as a special training session would be provided for overseas volunteers on arrival in Atlanta.

Volunteers at the games did not get any expenses, and had to arrange their own accommodation and travel. An Atlanta rental agent found me a bed and breakfast place in another town, Buckhead, which is about a one hour journey from Atlanta. The cost was around a hundred pounds per night. Most of the rooms in the city of Atlanta cost much more, but by this time not much was available. The Olympics is a time when prices start to sky-rocket.

A return flight from London to Atlanta was quoted at £600. At the time my son was living in San Francisco, on the west coast of America. I asked how much a ticket to San Francisco would be, with a few days stop-over, followed by a flight to Atlanta, and return to UK; answer £500. It was a no-brainer; that was the option I went for. Amazing how you can take a far longer journey, by a few thousand miles, and end up saving £100. Airline ticket costings are a complete mystery .

A short time later I received the training package. It consisted of a manual and video tape and was certainly very thorough and motivational. As I worked my way through the training material, I got a feeling of increasing excitement and anticipation. Yes, this was the Olympic Games and I was actually going to play a part in them.

The first modern Olympiad had taken place in Athens in 1896, a hundred years before. These Games were designated the Atlanta Centenary Olympic Games, or ACOG. The Atlanta committee pledged to:

1) Conduct the games with sensitivity, integrity, fiscal responsibility and commitment to the needs of athletes.

2) Share with the world the spirit of America, the experience of the American South and the vision of Atlanta.

3) Leave a positive, physical and spiritual legacy and an indelible mark upon Olympic history by staging the most memorable games ever.

It was clear that as volunteers we had a big part to play in the success of the games. In Los Angeles in 1984 there were thirty thousand volunteers, in Barcelona in 1992 there were thirty-five thousand, and in Atlanta in 1996 they planned to have forty-five thousand. The book said "No other Olympic Games in history have depended on volunteers to this extent. It is our chance to show the world the power of volunteerism". Certainly a new word to add to the dictionary.

In 2012 the London Olympic Games will need more than seventy thousand, double the Barcelona number. In twenty years that is a big increase, although since the tragedy of 9/11 the need for people in a security role will have grown considerably.

Very detailed plans were given with all the major Olympic venues listed. An area defined as 'The Olympic Ring', an imaginary circle with a radius of 1.5 miles, contained half a dozen major venues. The largest were the Olympic Stadium which had 85,000 seats, and the Georgia Dome which had 72,000 seats. The dome could be divided, to provide two venues of 35,000 each, and was to be used mainly for gymnastics, basketball and handball.

In the past when other countries had hosted the Olympic Games, their governments had provided the greater part of the cost. It is said that it took thirty years for Montreal to finally pay back the debt for the Games held in 1976.

The total budget for the Atlanta Games was quoted in the training manual as $1.7 billion. It was the proud boast of the organisers that sponsors provided, directly or indirectly, 70% of the costs of the Atlanta Centenary Olympic Games. To recognise their contribution, volunteers were directed to take special care to refrain from using or displaying any product or logo which belonged to a competitor of the sponsors.

The Coca Cola organisation has its corporate headquarters in Atlanta, and was clearly one of the biggest contributors to the Olympic Games. You would certainly have had great difficulty in finding a bottle of Pepsi Cola anywhere in town due to the dominance of Coca Cola, and to use anything but a Visa card also caused problems.

We were also provided with a mass of gee-whizz statistics, in order to satisfy the curiosity of visitors to The Games who might ask us questions. The Olympic village would provide housing for 14,000 athletes, coaches and team officials. There were more than 100 media outlets for TV, radio and press. Atlanta had invested more than $500 million in venue construction.

There was a neat little Olympic Games pocket fact book provided as a ready reference for all staff. It told us that there were 10,600 athletes expected to compete, 6,700 male and 3,900 female. Twenty six sports events were competed for, with 271 medal events. It listed the 197 countries competing. The new sports to be included for the first time were beach volleyball, mountain bike racing and softball.

To put the location in perspective three million people live in metropolitan Atlanta. The state of Georgia is the fourth state of the USA, it was named after George I I of England and is the 21st largest state.

There were guidelines to help volunteers to deal with security problems. Generally the message was, if there is a problem find a security man wearing a white shirt and green pants and tell him. If there are protestors and demonstrators don't try to handle it yourself, find the security man.

If you receive a request for political asylum from athletes or visitors find a security or law enforcement officer and he must contact Immigration. I was quite relieved that none of these things actually happened to me.

The overall message was "make every minute count". I certainly intended to.

Before travelling, I contacted the Bristol Evening Post, my local paper, to offer my services as a temporary reporter. They said that as they would not have any representation in Atlanta, they would like me to send back any news on the progress of the west-country competitors. I was provided with a list of all their names and events.

They sent a reporter and photographer to talk to me at home and printed an article and picture in the evening paper about my big adventure. Under my photograph the text read:

"'Sporting Honour..... Bristol sports fan Mike Cooper is to represent Britain in this summer's Olympic Games...as an usher".

The BBC in Bristol also invited me in take part in a live interview. Things were getting exciting.

Atlanta Olympic Games 1996

Tuesday 16th July

The first thing that hit me when I got off the plane in Atlanta was the heat; it was absolutely sweltering. The airport looked very spruce and well prepared for the most important three weeks Atlanta will ever know. A clear message displayed was "the world is coming to Atlanta". The whole place was buzzing with a party atmosphere, and a real Southern State welcome to all visitors was provided by the friendly, hospitable volunteer staff. This was where I met my first volunteers. They were instantly recognisable by their uniforms. The most impressive feature was the trilby style hat, with Atlanta 1996 embroidered on a blue band. There was however an air of strict security with many metal detectors being used, and staff carrying out handbag searches and frisking new arrivals.

I introduced myself to one of the Olympic volunteer staff, and was informed that regardless of whether one was a competitor, coach, official or volunteer, everything started with accreditation. This lady volunteer took me to collect my baggage and directed me to the bus.

At the Accreditation Centre I lined up in a queue alongside the Hungarian national team, complete with a film crew photographing every movement of their team members. Whether they mistook me for a national athlete or not I don't know but the camera swung in my direction once or twice, so I might be better known in Hungary than I was at home!

After a short wait my photograph was taken, personal details filled in and an identity card complete with a chain was hung around my neck. Also attached to the chain was a special card allowing free transport within the city of Atlanta via the transport service known as MARTA, and a second card which could be used in any vending machine to get a free drink, for the period of the games. Oh boy! I could drink as much as I liked for three weeks and it wouldn't cost a dime. Mind you, it was so hot in Atlanta that we were reminded that it was important to drink large volumes of liquid. I think the recommendation was 2 litres of water each day.

The accreditation procedure was a very slick and efficient operation managed by friendly staff.

Accreditation completed, it was time to find my lodgings for the duration of the games, which were in Buckhead. The travelling time was about one and a half hours from the main stadium. I phoned my hostess, Janice, which is pronounced Jan..eece, and arranged to meet her an hour later. This was the first opportunity to try out the free MARTA train card. It was very straight forward, simply putting the card into the turnstile and getting onto the next train.

I met Janice at the station she took me to her home. It was a very nice house, I just wished it could have been an hour nearer to the centre of activities. She was a delightful black American lady, with a splendid Southern accent. There were times when she used expressions, and said things that I found quite difficult to understand first time and had to ask her to repeat. I am sure she thought I was either deaf or daft or both, but after a short time I managed to get my ear tuned in and we had a bit of a joke about it. There was one place name, en route to the Stadium, that I could never pronounce properly even after a couple of weeks, it is called Wyucca.

My first call the next morning was to get my uniform from a depot at Dekatur. My attempt at pronunciation failed miserably, when asking Janice for directions. She said she had never heard of the place, until I showed her the name on my instruction letter. She recognised it immediately, and gave me a totally different pronunciation; as someone once said, 'two nations divided by a common language'.

Atlanta Olympic Games 1996

Wednesday 17th July

The dress rehearsal for the opening ceremony was due in the evening, and I wanted to be involved in the Olympic Games as quickly as possible. A pre-requisite was to be properly dressed for the part in the volunteer's uniform. I took a train ride on the MARTA to the uniform issuing centre at Dekatur, and then a bus transfer. There was great camaraderie developing amongst all the volunteers, and there was a lively interest in which US state people came from; coming from the UK I was something of a novelty.

On the train I talked to Seth, a history teacher. He was expecting to host all the medal winners and the celebrities prior to the presentation ceremonies. To say that he was thrilled at the prospect was an understatement. Later on the bus I sat next to Wixey, who explained that she had to meet all the winning athletes after their event and arrange their TV interviews. It was amazing the range of responsibilities people had been offered at the Games. Everyone wanted to make sure they had the best role available, and I have to say I was absolutely delighted with mine.

The Volunteer uniform was issued from a vast warehouse on an industrial estate. When you entered they checked your credentials, and then you were escorted into an area for 'fitting'. It wasn't quite like going to a tailor's shop for measuring up. You tried on one of the handful of rather crumpled looking shirts lying on the trestle tables to determine whether you were small, medium, large, x-large or xx-large. It was a stiflingly hot day and there had been a bit of a walk from the bus, so most of the naked torsos trying on the shirts were glistening with fragrant perspiration. Each volunteer was issued with three shirts with a splendid design of green and gold hoops and leaves on a white background. Different classifications of volunteers had the same design although the colours varied. I seem to remember the medics for example had red rather than gold hoops and the track officials another colour.

Moving on you went through the same process with trousers. There were no confidential cubicles so several people were struggling in and out of the trousers, hopping around the floor from leg to leg. In all probability by the end of the games some five thousand men would have tried on any single garment. One wonders about the health and safety aspect of such an operation. Having established the size, everyone was issued with two pairs of long trousers made of heavy weight khaki drill. They bore the label of Haynes, the leading work-wear manufacturers in the US. I was to learn very quickly that long heavy-weight drill trousers might be ideal for working in a factory during the autumn and winter but worn in the stifling heat of an Atlanta summer they were incredibly uncomfortable and unbearably hot. In that type of heat it would have been kinder to offer an option to wear shorts.

We continued following a production line system through a series of halls where we collected the complete range of accessory items. Everything was embellished with the Olympic logo and 'Atlanta 1996'. There was a belt, and a generous sized belt bag (which the English might refer to as bum-bags but are known in America as fanny-bags). We were given three pairs of socks, a poncho to wear during the frequent torrential rain-storms, and a water bottle.

There was a magnificent trilby style hat made of a well aerated airtex type of resin material. There was only one size, but each hat had an elasticated inner band so that it would fit a variety of heads. Some form of headwear was essential protection in view of the blistering sun. During the latter stages of the games there were press rumours that souvenir hunters of Olympic memorabilia had offered as much as fifteen hundred dollars for one of these hats. If anyone had offered me that amount of money I would have grabbed it, as it would have paid off my flight and other expenses handsomely.

Another much sought after souvenir item was a special wrist watch supplied by Swatch, one of the Centennial Games Olympic Partners. It carried all the Olympic logos and told the time precisely.

There was one other item to be collected from a different location; the special Olympic shoes.

So apart from underpants the volunteer was clothed completely from head to foot in the Olympic uniform.

Carrying all the gear in a plastic bag, we had a long walk followed by a long wait for the next bus to the station. By this time it was nearing midday and the sun was at its hottest. There followed a MARTA ride to Plaza Centre where I was told I could get details of the Volunteer training that was taking place later. However, nobody there seemed to have any idea where it was happening and I was constantly being sent from one person to another. This was before the days of personal mobile phones.

I met up with two younger volunteers, Kevin and Pete who said they were on a training session later that evening at the main stadium and they were able to direct me to the appropriate office. A few days later I met them again outside the stadium. When I asked them how things were going they replied glumly that they had been thrown off the volunteer team and their accreditation badge had been taken away. Their crime was that they had been seen lounging round chewing gum while on duty. High standards were expected from volunteers.

Somewhere on the way to the stadium there was a large digital clock over the roadway, counting down the last days, hours, minutes and seconds to the Opening Ceremony. It had been there for a couple of years ticking off the seconds for the benefit of the Atlanta commuters. It was rapidly nearing zero hour.

Everywhere around the stadium there were construction workers, scaffolders, carpenters and painters moving with unaccustomed haste for people in the building business, trying to complete the last minute jobs to meet the deadline two days later. In making my way to the stadium I was directed to the wrong MARTA station, and had to retrace my footsteps and go to another station. With all the train and bus journeys I was grateful to have the free travel card; so far on this day alone I would have accumulated about £30 worth of travel. Then there was a long walk to an office only to be told to go somewhere else. This was really the pattern of things prior to the opening ceremony; lots of enthusiastic amateurs with little or no information about what was going on. No one had any experience of the job they were doing; everyone had to learn as they went along. I guess that is the nature of a volunteer role in the Olympic Games, few have done it before and few are ever likely to do it again.

Eventually I was directed to a tent where the training was supposed to be happening; another snag – my name wasn't on the list. This meant another walk around the stadium to find the queries section where at last I found someone who knew who I was and could provide the training necessary. His name was Gene, a management level volunteer, who had worked for my old company. I had already spoken to him on the phone from England. I was still dressed in my own clothes and was carrying all my volunteer uniform in a bag. He said if I changed into uniform, he would give me the essential training so that I could be in the stadium, on duty for the dress rehearsal of the opening ceremony later that evening. Attendance at the rehearsal would ensure that I could attend the real opening ceremony on the Friday night forty-eight hours later.

Most of the volunteers in the main stadium had already been to training sessions earlier in the summer. They had been on duty at the trials to select the members of the USA team. The method of selecting the American team was very straightforward; the first three competitors in each event were chosen regardless of other circumstances. If the greatest performer in the world didn't make the first three on that day he would not be selected, for whatsoever reason.

Volunteers living outside the US were invited to attend these trials for training, although the authorities were sympathetic if we couldn't make it, as that would have meant an additional expensive flight. Gene had already agreed during a phone call from the UK that he would provide special training when I reached Atlanta.

The training was well handled and efficient. I had received my very comprehensive manual about three months previously which covered most of the essential points. One instruction they did strongly emphasise was that pointing with the fingers is considered offensive in many cultures. To indicate a direction you should use the open hand palm up. Failure to do this could offend the people of at least fourteen different nations.

To greet a small group or individuals the suggested approach would be to say 'Hello, my name is Cindy-Lou and I want to welcome you to the Olympic Stadium. Is there anything I can do to make your visit more enjoyable?' This is admirable in a tranquil setting with just a few people around. However when faced with a long queue (or 'line' as the Americans call it), with hundreds of people impatiently trying to get to their seats you tended to abbreviate your greeting to say something like 'tickets please'.

We were told to avoid expressions like 'cool' and 'you bet'. This was really no problem to me personally, as they were not part of my normal vocabulary. We were also told to avoid offering personal opinions about local conditions such as the weather. Imagine a volunteer at the London Olympics being told not to say 'lovely day' or 'it's a bit cooler today'

For a volunteer to cheer or applaud any performance was regarded as a cardinal sin. The reason given was that the athlete you applauded might have just beaten another whose relatives were sitting nearby. I wondered whether I would be able to contain myself if I witnessed a gold winning performance by a British star. I needn't have worried; sadly it didn't happen.

Having passed the training requirements we were taken into the main stadium so we understood the seating arrangements. I experienced a terrific feeling of excitement on entering this wonderful arena. The seating capacity was about eighty-four thousand, with seats on four different levels. The heat was quite oppressive at the lower levels, although higher up it was cooler and more pleasant as the air could circulate. The centre was covered in blue polythene sheeting, so we couldn't actually see the running track. We were briefed on our duties for the evening-essentially checking visitors' tickets and showing them where to sit.

Volunteers and their families who were working in all the other locations had been given tickets for the rehearsal. My first job was to stand at the end of a tunnel and check the tickets. The first two hours were hectic, with long queues building up and stretching down the steps. Everybody was cooperative and in good spirits, and tolerant of the stadium staff who were doing the job for the first time at this venue. We were all volunteers after all. A big problem was that many of the spectators wanted to leave their seats and wander all over the stadium and this was not permitted. Once the majority had found their places and had settled down for the start there was a torrential rain storm, and as very little of the seating was under cover, everybody left their seats and rushed back past our ticket post to find some shelter. The ceremony was delayed for a short while, until the deluge stopped, then everyone returned to their places, which meant re-checking their tickets. Their seats by this time were thoroughly wet.

When things got under way again there were a lot of trumpeters and other members of bands marching through the gangways between the seats playing rousing tunes, and each block of seats had glamorous cheerleaders ensuring a high level of response from the spectators. The ceremony was spectacular and very colourful with a magnificent ballet dance troupe covering the whole of the centre arena dressed as butterflies, waving their enormous ten foot span silver wings. There were large trailers towed by cars around the track carrying percussionists playing big silver oil drums.

This part of the ceremony was highly entertaining, but the subsequent parts did not have a great deal of spectator appeal. It was impossible in a rehearsal to simulate a realistic entry of all ten thousand athletes marching round the stadium to gather in the centre of the arena. The true competitors were too busy completing the last stages of their training to come to a rehearsal march and then stand around the centre of the arena for a couple of hours. In spite of their absence it was important for the organisers to get some idea of timings and space requirements, so all the teams were represented by a young girl bearing a card with the name of the country, a volunteer carrying the national flag, another volunteer holding one end of a length of string, and another volunteer some way back holding the other end. The length of the string was estimated to represent the size of that national team. So for the larger teams like Russia and the USA, there would be maybe a hundred yards of string separating first to last athletes. Watching nearly two hundred countries represented as lengths of string marching past in this way wasn't really very gripping, and took nearly an hour. When all the string was gathered and suitably distributed around the centre of the arena, the Olympic oath was taken by an anonymous volunteer, and the Olympic hymn was sung.

William Porter Payne, generally known as Billy Payne, the President and Chief Executive Officer of the Atlanta Olympic Committee gave a speech thanking all the volunteers, saying there were eighty thousand people in the stadium and telling them that the success of the Games depended to a large extent on their participation. He said that the count down to the Official Opening Ceremony was now one day, twenty three hours ...and counting.

The arrival of the mock Olympic torch carried by an unknown volunteer jogging around the track, was followed by the mimed lighting of the flame. No one knew who would actually light the flame on the opening night; it was a very closely guarded secret. There was a great deal of speculation among the spectators as to the identity of the sportsmen who would have the honour of carrying the Olympic torch into the stadium, around the track and actually lighting the flame. Favoured names were Ed Moses, the 400 metre hurdler who had an unbeaten run of over one hundred races, and Bruce Jenner, the winner of the Decathlon event in 1976. We would just have to wait and see.

The rehearsal ended with a fireworks display, not quite as grand as the one two days later, but nevertheless pretty good.

The final task for the stadium volunteers was to clear the rows of seats, move people out and check for valuables left behind. We then had a de-brief with our group leaders and received our instructions for the real Opening Ceremony two days later.

On the train home I was travelling with a group of volunteer girls from the local college who were responsible for carrying the country name cards in front of the national teams in the opening ceremony. One of them was carrying the card for Virgin Islands, and was particularly excited because she expected that they would be lining up next to the heroes from her own country, the USA team, in the alphabetical sequence.

Not everyone was fortunate enough to be assigned to the main stadium The opening ceremony rehearsal did give the volunteers who were to be employed at some of the less glamorous locations a chance to witness the bigger picture and to enjoy the feeling of camaraderie with the other volunteers.

I went home with a great feeling of excitement and anticipation.

Atlanta Olympic Games 1996

Thursday 18th July

The only remaining part of my uniform that I had not collected were the shoes, which for some reason were not issued at the same place as the rest of the clothing. As most volunteers had been issued with their uniforms in the preceding weeks, they had run out of most of the popular sizes. After trying several of the larger, and smaller sizes I eventually found a pair that were comfortable, which was a good thing as the stadium volunteers spent most of the day standing; sitting on duty was strictly frowned upon. They were a splendid design manufactured by Reebok. The Olympic Games logo and the words 'Authentic Olympic Games Collection', were embroidered on a label on the tongue of the shoe. They were well up to the high standards of the rest of the uniform.

Although I had received some training the day before, I had been told to come back again for what they called 'venue training'. The volunteers who were resident in the state of Georgia had already received their venue training, but a few from outside the state still needed to go through the process.

Before leaving home I had been sent the very comprehensive self-study training manual covering in detail the role of volunteer staff. It gave a brief history and an overview of the Centennial Games and answers to questions you might be asked about the organisation, leaders and various symbols you might see. It went into some detail about the different venues; how to find them, their capacity, and competitive events that would take place there. The message from the training manual that I still remember most clearly, many years later is 'Make every moment count'.

When I had flown all the way to Atlanta, paid for my own accommodation, and was privileged to be part of the greatest event in the world, then I really did want to enjoy every moment, and to meet as many people from different countries and walks of life as possible. I didn't want to miss anything worth seeing.

The venue training was scheduled for 3.0 pm, and at that time the heat was intense, and the MARTA train system was bursting at the seams. I arrived at the station late, and had to run all the way to the training session. At this time I was wearing the Volunteer uniform, and I found it horribly uncomfortable running in heat in excess of 100 degrees. I arrived at the training venue late and feeling uncomfortably hot and clammy. Being late didn't really matter, as it eventually started at least an hour after I got there.

Amongst other things we were given instructions for the procedure for the medal ceremonies. It was in the form of a memo from Carter Parsley, the ACOG Assistant Program Manager – Victory Ceremony.

' ACOG has no official protocol regarding staff playing of national anthems, but the appropriate procedure according to the Georgia Department of Industry, Trade and Tourism is:

-Staff rise for the playing of all anthems (U.S. and foreign)

-Staff remove hats or other cover during the playing of all anthems (U.S. and foreign)

-Hand over heart for the U.S. national anthem is optional.

-Flow of foot traffic into and out of seating areas stops during the playing of all anthems.

Each awards ceremony will begin with a trumpet fanfare introduction. Award winners will enter the field. An announcement will be made, "Please rise for the national anthem of (country) Staff then rises and removes head cover."

Nice to know that the Department of Industry, Trade and Tourism could tell us exactly what we had to do during a medal ceremony.

The rest of the venue training amounted to a guided walk around the stadium learning where all the blocks of seats were, so you could direct people to the right area if they came in the wrong entrance. Some of the seat numbering was a little bit confusing. But it was a great moment to be able to stand back to look at the magnificent 85000-seater stadium and just marvel at it. The massive cauldron which would hold the Olympic flame during the games towered above everything. The bowl stood 110 feet above the ground, weighed 8 tons, and was made of 228 tons of steel. It would be lit the following day by the celebrity whose name at this time was still a closely guarded secret. The massive flame would then be visible for miles around the city to proclaim that the games were in progress. It would be lit by the torch that had been ignited from the sun's rays at Mount Olympus some months before and was at that moment approaching the city of Atlanta.

After we had completed the venue training the next thing I wanted to do was to find out where the Olympic torch had got to, and watch it go past.

The torch had been carried by an estimated ten thousand people, through forty-two of the states during the last eighty-four days. It had been on horse-back, on canoes, trains and any other form of transport that enterprising people could think of. Former athletes, politicians, schoolchildren and many of the great and the good of the USA had been honoured by carrying it a few yards towards its final destination.

I had met Kim, another IBM employee volunteer at the training who offered me a lift to try to locate the torch along its planned route. When we thought we were getting close we were soon completely surrounded by the crowds, and unable to drive at a sensible speed. Everyone in Atlanta had decided to watch the progress of the Olympic Torch. We hastily abandoned the car and stood by the roadside to await arrival of the flame. The police were really struggling to control the crowds but there was a great party atmosphere. When the torch bearer eventually reached us he was three hours behind schedule. First the police motor cycle escort followed by the bus carrying some of the other torch bearers crawled towards us. No one in the crowd moved to let them past, the police motor cyclists had to nudge a way through.

The current torch bearer was some way behind surrounded by more police, travelling at a hesitant slow walking pace, as everyone in the crowd tried to reach out to touch the torch. Eventually we were able to return to the car and work our way through the carnival crowds. Later as we passed the digital clock by the roadway on our way home, it was slowly but surely decrementing to zero hour,

Yes, with the Olympic torch so close to the stadium you could feel that the Centenary Olympic Games had really arrived.

Atlanta Olympic Games 1996

Friday 19th July

The volunteers were on duty three hours before the scheduled start of the Opening Ceremony, allowing time to get everybody to their seats. I was part of Bruce's team, and we were working in the area next to the VIP seats.

About twenty security guards the size of Mike Tyson frisked the spectators for metal objects at the entrance to our section. The average American attending a sports event liked to carry a case full of camera gear, a tripod, and a cool box loaded with cans of beer. The process of checking for weapons was not easy. Since 9/11 we have come to accept these procedures as normal at airports and public events, but in the halcyon days of 1996 security was not such an issue. When the spectators had satisfied the guards that they were just harmless sports fans the stadium staff checked the tickets, before showing them to their seats. Many tickets had cost over $600, (about £400), however on the streets outside 'scalpers' were rumoured to be selling them at five-times that price.

There were eighty-six thousand spectators in the stadium for the opening ceremony. A further two billion were watching on television. The nations' leaders and Olympic dignitaries from all over the world were there. Our team of volunteers was in the section just in front of the BBC and the VIP area, where President Clinton, Antonio Samaranch, President of the Olympic committee and the great and the good from the world of politics and sport were gathered. The atmosphere was electric; you could almost reach out and touch the excitement.

Due to traffic snarl-ups and security concerns, everything was running half an hour late. There had been traffic delays as not all drivers knew their way around Atlanta; there were also volunteers coming from many other states of the USA. Eventually when all the punters were seated, the stadium staff had to ensure that the gangways were kept clear. This provided us with the opportunity to find a good viewing point. We were in a perfect position to witness the truly breath-taking spectacle of the Opening Ceremony.

Many say that the Olympic Games are the 'Greatest Show on Earth', and I whole-heartedly agree. This was the start of the twenty most exciting days of my life.

As I said before, I had been assigned to the role of 'stadium management'. A grand title; what did it mean? In fact it really boiled down to being an usher, checking tickets and directing the spectators to their seats - wow! - the Olympic Stadium - what a place to do it. Two hundred other fortunate ushers shared this plum assignment.

We all looked immaculate in the volunteer's uniform; a shirt with distinctive green and yellow hoops, khaki slacks, and to crown it a magnificent Southern States style hat, with a broad blue band embroidered 'Atlanta 1996'

The first part of the programme was a fifteen million dollar artistic extravaganza. Five buggies with oversized balloon-wheels drove around the track, each carrying oil-drum percussion bands, which belted out their Caribbean rhythms. Then the arena filled with hundreds of singing children, their angelic faces peering out of white ruffles like little lilies. Dancers with enormous silver wings moved gracefully like dragonflies on a summer's-day. Mingling with them were twelve-foot high stilt walkers, in elaborate shimmering white costumes. Next a troupe of gladiators appeared carrying long cylindrical pillars; using these they erected six large screens forming a hexagon. From within, silhouettes of ancient Greeks were projected onto the white fabric as gracefully they mimed different athletic events in slow motion. The hors-d'oeuvre of artistic talent over, it was time for the main course.

A dozen of America's elite marines marched into the arena, holding taut the unfolded Olympic flag. The five distinctive inter-locking rings, representing the five continents, were facing up to the heavens. It was paraded to the flagpole and ceremonially raised, to flutter symbolically in the gentle breeze. The solemn singing of the Olympic hymn by a massed choir was followed by the American National anthem. Witnessing thousands of American citizens, hands held across hearts, loyally singing the 'Star Spangled Banner' is a stirring experience, regardless of your own nationality.

The parade of nearly two hundred national teams lasted for almost two hours. Each team was led by a local schoolgirl displaying a placard showing the name of the country, followed by the chosen figurehead holding their national flag. Some of the smaller nations might have as few as half a dozen representatives, others ran to hundreds. One could not help feeling considerable pride and not a little emotion to see the British team in smart trilby hats with the girls in neat check shorts. Steve Redgrave, who a few days later was to achieve a magnificent fourth gold medal in his fourth Olympiad, marched all the way around the track with the Union Jack held in his outstretched arm.

Finally, as host nation, the American team entered the stadium, far outnumbering all the others. The response of the home crowd was absolutely deafening. Their full-blooded roar lasted for several minutes as the team marched - or skipped- round the track to take up their place in the centre of the arena.

There had been serious delays as not all team bus-drivers knew their way around Atlanta; they were also volunteers, coming from many other states of the USA. It was comical to watch some of the American late-comers charging helter-skelter down the ramp to make up the fifty yard gap that had developed between them and the rest of their team.

Once the athletes had gathered in the centre the speeches began. The Olympic President Juan Antonio Samaranch, welcomed the 'Youth of the World' to the Centenary Olympic Games. At 64 the Puerto Rican rifle team-member must have felt great pride to be included amongst them. A Slovenian gymnast, still looking fit at 94, was introduced as the oldest living past-Olympian. The Olympic Oath was solemnly taken on behalf of the athletes by Teresa Edwards a female American basketball player; sadly this was to be the last time that the Olympic Oath was taken without any reference to drug taking. Then Hobie Billingsley, a renowned American diver and respected coach took the Oath on behalf of the judges.

There was an interlude set aside for audience participation. Every spectator had received a goodie-bag which included a torch, a scarf and a piece of card entitled 'Audience Stunt Summary'. When prompted by the giant screen, everyone had to shout out 'Welcome, Welcome, Welcome'.

The scarves came in several different colours and on the command all spectators waved them obediently above their heads. The stadium blossomed into a palette of vivid colour. Then all the lights were turned off and the giant screen commanded 'Go -- colour flashlights'. The lens on each torch was covered by a different colour. We switched on and followed the actions of the section leader, moving the multi-coloured lights in great big circles. For a completely unrehearsed audience it was well disciplined and very effective. The instruction went up 'shine your lights at the blimp'. The television cameras in the blimp, hovering a thousand feet above, relayed the kaleidoscopic panorama for the rest of the world to savour.

Visa was one of the dozen or so sponsors, and everyone was given a card with an opening balance of $5 in the goodie-bag. The gift was very welcome, although if you could afford $636 for a seat, did you really need that five bucks? Kodak, another sponsor provided a small disposable camera for every spectator.

Undoubtedly the arrival of the Olympic torch was the pinnacle of the opening ceremony. There is always speculation at any Olympiad about the identity of the sportsman chosen to light the Olympic flame. As the torch approached the stadium we learnt that the athlete to bring it into the stadium was Al Oerter, who had won the discus in four consecutive Olympiads in the fifties and sixties. He carried the torch through the underground passages below the stadium, which was a bit unfortunate for him as he was out of sight of the spectators in the stadium. He emerged from a trap door in the centre of the track where the spotlight picked him out for a few fleeting seconds before he handed over the flaming torch to Evander Holyfield who had won a bronze medal in the boxing in 1984. He was very much a local hero having held the world heavy-weight boxing title.

Evander Holyfield jogged part-way round the track to be joined by a female athlete who we learnt was Paraskevi Patoulidou. She was the first ever woman from Greece to win a gold medal, which she did in the 100 metre hurdles in 1992.They jogged together for halfway round the track, before handing over to Janet Evans, the US swimming legend who had won four gold medals. Janet set off up a very long slope leading to the giant cauldron, where the Olympic flame would burn for the duration of the games.

We had almost reached the climax of the evening. As she ran up a long steep ramp, the huge score-board lit up with the name 'Muhammad Ali Gold Medallist Boxing 1960'.

The spotlight picked out the unmistakeable profile of 'The Greatest'. To a standing ovation he accepted the flame with his right hand, his left shaking violently. With difficulty he thrust the torch into a small aperture at knee-height, and for several seconds the flame climbed slowly but steadily along the fuse to the top of a tall gantry. Then -whoosh- the symbolic red bowl burst into flame. This burning cauldron of fire would dominate the stadium for the duration of the Games. There was a roar of applause from everyone in the stadium; this signified the start of a wonderful three weeks of intense competition. It was also a moment of enormous emotion, tinged with great sadness that such a magnificent physical specimen had succumbed to the ravages of Parkinson's Disease. It was an experience that the thousands of spectators will remember for the rest of their lives.

The announcer said, "We hope every athlete will feel the power of the dream" and the spotlight turned onto the French-Canadian singer Celine Dion. She looked delightfully elegant, in a long white dress, while her accompanist played the grand piano behind her, with the full Olympic choir standing on a long steep ramp alongside. She sang 'The Power of the Dream' with tremendous energy and power with the choir swaying from side to side with the rhythm, and the athletes in the centre waving and also moving to the rhythm. I marvelled at the way a singer could perform so passionately on a stage in front of a live audience of more than eighty thousand plus a couple of billion viewers at home. Celine was brilliant.

The words of the song 'the world unites in hope and peace', was particularly poignant as this was the first Olympiad when all the 197 nations were represented. In the past there had been boycotts for some reason or another. The ancient Greeks would stop all wars for the duration of the Olympics, we should learn from them.

There followed the grand finale, a spectacular fireworks display, the finest and most extravagant I had ever been privileged to watch. It must have lasted for a good half an hour, and the sky was a blaze of colour.

Once the ceremony was over, the stadium staff had the last duty of the day to carry out. We had to sweep through the rows of seats in search of any lost property, bombs or people who had fallen asleep.

Leaving the stadium, we passed what was probably the largest stretch-limo in the cosmos, dwarfing all the other gargantuan American gas-guzzlers around it. The number plate said quite simply' HOLY 1' The locals said it belonged to the boxer Evander Holyfield, although one wonders what Mohammed Ali's number plate was.

Atlanta Olympic Games 1996

Saturday 20th July

After the excitement of the Opening Ceremony, there was no activity planned for the stadium until the following Friday. This meant that the stadium volunteers had nearly a week without any formal duties to enjoy the other sporting competitions taking place around the city.

The official place to get tickets for any event was the Peach Tree Centre in town, so I went there with a view to seeing the hockey games where both the British men's and women's teams were competing. There were some sports competitions that I had never seen before, and thought weight-lifting and water-polo would be interesting to watch.

There was a short queue just outside the building, so I joined expecting it would be just a few minutes wait. After about half an hour of shuffling forward we got inside the building where the queue crossed the hall, and disappeared into a door. Fortunately there were some quite interesting people around me to talk to including an Argentinian couple from Buenos Aires. Like me, he belonged to the Rotary Club, so this gave us quite a lot of common topics to discuss, and his English was pretty good. As my job at this time was teaching English to business executives, he was grateful to me for helping him with one or two grammatical points. This may seem a bit sad, but it did help to pass the time in a queue. He did mention the Falkland War but as it had been over for more than ten years it was no longer a serious issue with him.

No sooner had we moved from the first hall than we found that the queue there stretched across another room to disappear into a doorway. We continued shuffling through different doors until after three and a half hours we entered the room where the ticket counters where located.

It was a sorry sight. There were groups of forlorn potential purchasers sitting on the floor looking disgruntled and bored. Some of the staff behind the counter were tapping keys and peering into their computer screens more in hope than expectation; others were reading or chatting to each other. The reason we were given for the appallingly long delay was that the computer was down. Oh dear! Was it the much vaunted IBM computer which was responsible?

After another half hour or so, a half-hearted cheer went up; the computer was working again. I managed to get a couple of tickets for the men's and women's hockey matches featuring the Great Britain teams.

Shortly after leaving the ticket office, I met someone who had abandoned the ticket queue after half an hour and had managed to buy tickets from a scalper, paying only a few dollars over the official price. The transaction was completed in a couple of minutes. Maybe there was a lesson there.

This was the first day of the Olympic competition and bits of news started to filter through the grapevine. The honour of winning the first gold medal went to Renata Mauer of Poland in the shooting event. One of the stories that we heard was that the defending Judo medallist from Georgia reported to the wrong venue and was disqualified. There was also a rumour that the computer system that was supposed to be producing the results for the press wasn't doing what it should be doing.

To get to the hockey competition I had to take the MARTA train system, which was beginning to feel the strain of the sudden increase in traveller traffic, with long queues everywhere. On arrival at the station, I asked an official where the hockey ground was. He looked at me in amazement and said that there was no ice rink anywhere near that part of the city. I showed him my ticket for the Alonzo Herndon Stadium and all was explained. To the Americans hockey means only one thing - ice-hockey. What we would call hockey in Britain, they call field-hockey.

All the hockey games were played at the Alonzo Herndon Stadium which was on the campus of the Atlanta University Centre. The sports facilities generally at American universities are absolutely magnificent, and this hockey field was no exception. The illuminated scoreboard behind the goals kept the spectators informed on the game's progress, with a few comic figures to add a bit of humour to the serious activities on the pitch. The artificial pitch looked immaculate, and when the sun went down behind the stand by the side of the pitch, the blood red sky was sensational.

On a visit to California a few years previously, I went to the American Football stadium at Stanford University which can hold seventy to eighty thousand spectators. In fact the facilities were so good that it was used to host some soccer games in the World Cup competition. The American university gymnasia, swimming pools and tennis courts provide really outstanding spectator and performer facilities. It is a wonder to me that British athletes can perform so well competing on the world stage when many have to train with such Spartan and ill-funded facilities.

There were a few hundred British supporters for the hockey teams and plenty of Union Flags in evidence. Unfortunately the ladies hockey team lost to South Korea by 5-0. Sue Slocombe the British team manager said afterwards, 'we didn't play badly, but were beaten by a good South Korean team.'

Atlanta Olympic Games 1996

Sunday 21ˢᵗ July

The women's cycling road race started early on a Sunday morning. It consisted of 8 laps of 8.1 miles around the local streets, for a total of 64.8 miles. During the two and a half hour event there was a typical Atlanta rain-storm leaving the roads wet and slippery. Competitors who had conscientiously prepared for the hot sweltering climate, found themselves racing in relatively cool and wet conditions.

The cycling road races were a good opportunity for the local community to enjoy an Olympic final on their home roads, and there was no charge for the privilege. It was estimated that about 50,000 spectators watched the event. Right at the back of the race was a large van following the last girl competing and ready to rescue any one in trouble. It had broom-heads attached across the front bumper, (or fender as the Americans would call it), and was referred to as the 'broom wagon'.

The gold medal was won by the oldest competitor in the race, 37 year-old, Jeannie Longo-Ciprelli from France, who beat Imelda Chiappi of Italy by 25 seconds. Longo-Cipprelli had an outstanding competitive record having been world road race champion five times, and had competed in the Olympics four times. She had been a competitive skier when younger, but didn't make the French team so turned to cycling. In 2008 she was in Beijing competing in her eighth Olympics finishing fourth in the road race. Who knows she might even delay retirement so she can compete at London 2012 for number nine.

The medal ceremony after the race was the first of many that I was privileged to watch during the Games. Above the finishing line of the race there was a gantry some fifteen feet high with boards displaying 'Atlanta 1996', a time clock, and 'Finish'. In front of it there were three flagpoles, and a three tiered podium for the medal winners. Three pretty girls carrying trays with the gold, silver and bronze medals, marched out, followed by the official who was to make the awards, and of course the jubilant winners. The medals attached to ribbons embroidered with 'Atlanta 1996' were placed over their heads. They turned to face the flagpoles as the French National Anthem was played. There is nothing like watching the national flags of the medal winners being raised and the playing of a national anthem to bring a lump to the throat. With French and Italian medallists there was more than the usual level emotion and plenty of tears. If only it could have been 'God save the Queen'.

In the afternoon I went to watch the British men's hockey team playing against Korea in the preliminary rounds at the Alonzo Herndon Stadium. They had a large contingent of supporters with plenty of Union Flags in evidence. One British supporter had designed himself a full length Arab sheik robe from a large Union Jack, and was strutting purposefully amongst the British contingent. He looked very striking in his national outfit, and had attracted the attention of the television reporters, who had interviewed him on their programme.

When watching a 'British' team, the supporters shouting 'come on Great Britain' doesn't have the same resonance as the soccer supporters cheering on the England team. The word 'England' can be shouted or chanted with great passion and enthusiasm. Try shouting 'Great Britain' and it doesn't have the same snappy impact. When the hockey supporters tried to encourage the national team the words 'come on Great Britain' sounded a bit weak and disjointed. It just doesn't make music to the ear. Even If we used 'United Kingdom' it wouldn't be much of an improvement. Maybe we should find a new way to address our four-nation teams.

The British team were playing quite well and were leading 2-1 until the last two minutes when we gave away a penalty. I am unfamiliar with the finer points of gamesmanship in field hockey, but to my inexperienced, (and undoubtedly prejudiced) eye the Koreans did seem to indulge in diving to try to gain penalties.

When the Korean penalty taker stepped up to take the shot he called for a spray filled with water and then thoroughly drenched the ball. The British goalkeeper, Simon Mason, who must be several inches over six foot tall, watched these goings-on unfazed, then responded admirably with his own bit of gamesmanship. He stood on the goal line, a truly imposing figure, dressed in a yellow shirt, dark blue gauntlets with matching pads. He performed a high-kick, touching the cross bar just above his head with his left foot, did an about turn and kicked the bar with his right foot. Next he did the splits, facing first to the left, then the right; he stood up and stared hard at the penalty-taker. Gamesmanship and dramatics over, the Korean took the penalty. He scored. Result a 2-2 draw.

Among the spectators was a lady sporting a tee-shirt with 'I'm Simon Mason's Mum' printed on the back. She was the proud mother of the British goalkeeper, and came from Berkeley in Gloucestershire and I had a chance to talk to her afterwards. She said "It's so wonderful to be here, the spirit of Atlanta is brilliant. I'm so proud to be here, and the people of Berkeley are so proud too, they had a special Olympic window display in one of the shops". I asked her about the water-spraying incident and she replied "How strange to pour water on the ball, I've never seen that before" and with regard to Simon Mason's high kicks she simply said "Mase is ace"'.

Some of the British supporters thought the penalty was a bit harsh and moaned,"We was robbed".

There was a very surprising result in the Olympic soccer competition coming over the news channels. Japan beat Brazil 1-0.For a minor soccer nation to beat the mighty Brazilians could only happen in the Olympics.

An Interesting snippet printed in a local paper said Archbishop Desmund Tutu speaking at the service in a local Baptist Church exhorted Atlantans to help bring the 2004 Olympic Games to his country, South Africa. It didn't work – in 2004 the Olympic Games were held in Athens.

Mike Cooper

Atlanta Olympic Games 1996

Monday 22nd July

There are some sports in the Olympic programme that are not widely played in England. Water polo is rarely publicised or televised at home so I thought it would be worth watching, particularly as the best players in the world would be there.

Unlike the Georgia Aquatic Centre pool which had a roof over it, the water polo pool was in the open. It was a baking hot sunny afternoon. I was lucky in having a seat in a block with the sun behind my back. Those spectators on the other side of the pool were completely dazzled by the reflection on the water. There were three matches scheduled on the programme, Greece v Rumania, Croatia v Italy and Holland v Hungary, the latter being the best game finishing 10 goals to 8. It seemed to be a thoroughly exhausting game, as the swimmers appeared to spend all the game treading water, using a sort of bandy-legged ladder climbing motion, and then swimming frantically in short bursts to get the ball. The players had no hesitation in pushing their opponents under water, and the sort of foul play that went on below the surface beggars belief. They say that in water polo the real wars are fought below the surface, where the referee and spectators can't see what is going on. With the sun reflecting on the water, a low flying shot at goal ricocheting across the surface must have been impossible to follow by the goal keeper. Water polo did not attract a great following and there were many empty seats at the poolside, although in fairness it has to be said that these games were in the preliminary rounds.

On leaving the pool area, I was stopped by a TV reporter from the San Francisco channel, who wanted views about travelling within the city of Atlanta. At that stage I could not say that I had experienced any real problems with the transport system, most of my journeys had been pretty painless. This disappointed the reporter as he was clearly looking for something to entertain the faraway Californian viewers. However later in the week things did deteriorate. The MARTA rapid rail system consisted of a north-south line and a west-east line forming a sort of 'plus' sign. Where they intersected, the system really creaked under the sheer volume of passengers embarking, disembarking and changing trains. No doubt in the normal day-to-day activity of the city, it could cope, but when you import another million or so temporary visitors the workload becomes impossible. At one stage crowd controllers were stationed at the top and bottom of each escalator to prevent them becoming overloaded. People were being filtered very slowly onto the escalators by the security men, and big crowds of hot, cross and impatient travellers rapidly built up. I wonder how London will manage in 2012.

It was extremely hot in the streets, and the authorities did have some concern about the health of the visitors. The maximum temperature recorded in the city during this day was 95 degrees. There were kiosks where they were giving away white fabric protective sun hats, with a flap hanging down the neck at the back, rather like the kepis worn by the Foreign Legionnaires in Beau Geste. Drinking water was also available alongside notices warning people to take plenty of fluid; two litres a day seemed to be recommended. They had set up spray booths along the pavement where you could walk between a series of very fine cold jets of water to cool off. After the stifling heat of the streets these were delightfully refreshing.

In the evening I went to the Georgia Tech Aquatic Centre. It was vast, with seating for 15,000 spectators, which dwarfs the capacity of most other swimming venues in the world.

On the way from the water polo pool to the swimming pool, I saw a couple standing by the entrance holding an Irish flag. We started chatting and it turned out that they were the parents of Michelle Smith, who on the previous day had become the first woman ever to win a gold medal for Ireland, and her parents were justifiably very, very proud. She had won the 400 metres medley event, having beaten an American Alison Wagner. This was the first medal for swimming that Ireland had ever won. The proud parents posed for me for a photograph, waving the Irish flag with the inscription 'Michelle our belle.'

They told me that they had high hopes of her winning another gold medal in the final of the 400 metres freestyle later in the evening. The American favourite, Janet Evans who had won four gold medals in previous Olympiads had been eliminated in the heats earlier that day. Janet had been the final carrier of the Olympic torch at the opening ceremony, before handing over to Mohammed Ali when he lit the flame in the cauldron. There had been a good deal of speculation in the American press that Janet was on track for her fifth gold medal.

Four hundred metres is eight lengths of the pool, and after about six lengths Michelle seemed to be a couple of yards in front and stayed ahead to win. As there were no British competitors I was delighted to see an Irish victory. Half an hour after taking the first photo of her parents, I took my second photo of the jubilant couple, celebrating medal number two. There was no 50-metre Olympic-length swimming pool anywhere in Ireland, so Michelle and her Dutch husband had had to move to Holland to live so that she could train in a proper full-length pool.

She won a third gold in the 200 metre individual medley two days later, and followed that with a bronze medal by finishing third in the 200 metre butterfly stroke. It was an unbelievable achievement for Michelle, who up to that time had won more medals than swimmers from the two great swimming nations, Australia or Germany

President Bill Clinton went to the Olympic pool one day to meet Irish heroine Michelle Smith to congratulate her.

The highly vociferous home-based American spectators must have represented at least three quarters of the audience at the pool. Their stars and stripes flags predominated in a sea of colour, however just in front of me was a single Union Jack waving proudly and defiantly. I went to say hello, and to show solidarity with a fellow Brit, and the lady turned out to be the mother of the British swimmer James Hickman who had earlier qualified for the final of the 200 metres butterfly. He finished in seventh place in the final. She gave me a copy of a postcard which showed a photograph of James in action in the pool. On the back it gave a summary of his achievements; first Briton under two minutes for the 200 metres butterfly, and senior British and English record holder in that event. He had been Junior European champion in 1993.

In the women's backstroke event two swimmers from the USA finished first and second, and the home crowd went really wild, the sound was deafening in the enclosed arena. A prominent family group brandished a large flag with the words 'We love you Beth'; they were the supporters of Beth Botsford, winner of the gold medal in the backstroke, quite a performance for a fifteen year-old.

The excitement was repeated in the relay which was a very close run thing between USA and China. That evening there were 5 medal ceremonies, and although these are always emotional, the two involving the home competitors from the USA were particularly so, due to the sheer volume of home support. Performing in front of a home crowd is a massive advantage, although the pressure on the athlete not only to perform well, but to win something must be frightening.

A large group of some thirty members all wearing t-shirts bearing the logo 'Swim Malchow" were prowling around the arena in a pack letting their presence be known to intimidate the lesser mortals. Malchow of the USA went on to win a silver medal in the 200 metre butterfly event.

But proudest of all were the small Irish group of family and supporters of Michelle Smith holding the Irish flag, bearing a shamrock and the words 'Michelle Our belle' on it.

Atlanta Olympic Games 1996

Tuesday 23rd July

I had never watched weight-lifting as a competition event, so went along wondering if it would be much of a spectator sport. As it turned out it was very well presented and I found it absolutely thrilling.

There are two elements of the weight-lifting competition, the 'snatch' and the 'clean and jerk'. In the 'snatch' the lifter gets down into a squat position, grabs the bar and endeavours to pull the bar up above his head in an explosive flip movement; he needs to get his arms locked straight above his head. Then in a second movement he must straighten his legs, so he is standing with both legs firmly on the ground and arms straight with the weights above his head. Often the lifter has to struggle to get his balance by shuffling his feet around. The judges press a button to flash up a light when they are satisfied he is standing steadily on both feet. Each competitor gets three tries and as the competition progresses and the weights get heavier, the competitor can decide at which weight he wishes to take his three attempts.

In the 'clean and jerk' the bar is lifted from floor to shoulder height, held briefly, then pushed overhead in a second movement. In the same way the judges press the button when they are satisfied the competitor is steady. Heavier weights can be lifted using the 'clean and jerk' method.

The competitors came on to the stage and coated their hands generously with some sort of chalk powder from a large bowl. Then they approached the massive weights on the bar-bell lying on the floor. Some looked in the direction of the sky, or ceiling for inspiration or simply glowered at the stationary weights on the floor. The competitors had wide bandages tightly wrapped around both knees, seemingly to stop them falling apart under strain. Around the waist they wore a very wide heavy leather belt tightly strapped to hold in what was sometimes a very substantial stomach. The wrists were also covered in tight dusty bandages. Then slowly, very deliberately the competitor grasped the bar with hands more than shoulder width apart; after a moment of meditation with a sudden grunt, he lifted the bar up to his chest. The iron bar, loaded with heavy disks at each end, seemed almost unequal to the struggle as it bent into a shallow arc under the strain of the competing forces of the lifter's strength and the gravity force from the weighted disks. After a pause and another grunt he tried to raise the bar above his head, then straighten his arms and lock his knees.

The judges had to be satisfied that the lift had been properly completed, with the weights held aloft, and that the feet had stopped shuffling to find balance. The lifter would stand there with glazed eyes as he waited for the three judges to hit the button to light the bulb to say it is a good and fair lift. Sometimes this could take an agonisingly long time particularly as the judges would not give their approval until the lifter was absolutely steady. Then when the lights indicated that the lift was approved the weights were thrown to the floor where they clattered and bounced uncontrollably on the mat.

On other occasions the bar was raised without complete control and the lifter found that he had overcooked it, and he might stagger backwards, and fall onto his backside, or throw the weights in front of him and storm off the stage in disgust. It was a battle between the competitor and the bar loaded with dumb impersonal weights lying on the floor in front of him.

In the event for men weighing under 70kg the American competitor Tim McRae broke the US record by lifting 145kg, more than twice his body-weight. His family were there in large numbers and very vocal in their support. They had a large stars and stripes flag, a USA Olympic banner and several of them carried cards with such slogans as 'Tim McRae Daytona Beach', but proudest of all the supporters was a lady with a stars and stripes baseball cap, with a beaming smile and a card proudly proclaiming 'That's My Son'. In spite of the National record, poor old Tim only finished in fourteenth place.

For the medals the Chinese competitor Zhan Xugang and Kim Myong Nam from Korea were battling it out. Kim lifted 160kg at his third attempt, but Zhan managed to snatch 162.5kg to create a new world record. There was a tremendous ovation for this performance; it was very moving to witness a new world record, knowing that no one had ever achieved this weight in competition in the world before.

At the end of the event came the medal ceremony. The winners' rostrum was wheeled onto the stage and three girls with smart white hats and long dresses glided in gracefully, each with the tray containing either the gold, silver or bronze medal and bouquet of flowers for the medal winners. They started with the bronze medallist. He leapt onto the rostrum, and had his medal placed over his head to hang on his shoulders, and a bouquet thrust into his hands. To see these heavily muscled men holding a delicate bouquet of flowers seemed slightly incongruous. The silver medallist followed and finally the gold medal winner, who had to leap onto the highest platform. The national flags of China, Korea and Hungary were raised slowly and majestically in front of the medal winners as the Chinese national anthem was played. Americans like to do things in style, and these flags were enormous, they seemed to be about twenty feet long.

From the excitement and emotion of weightlifting, I moved on to the hockey stadium, where the British women's team were to play the USA team, on their home ground. A few days before the British team had played Korea in their first match and had been well and truly beaten by 5-0. Then they played Holland and drew.

Throughout, the home crowd were chanting USA, USA, USA, but the small contingent of British supporters responded enthusiastically doing their best to drown them. There was particularly vociferous support from a bunch of young people taking part in a Christian Fellowship summer camp, who were chanting, amongst other things, the words from 'Football's coming home'. The British supporters had a lot to cheer about when their team scored, and they held the lead till the final whistle to record a fantastic 1-0 victory over the Americans. Our supporters gave them a tumultuous reception at the end.

As I was acting as a part-time reporter for the Bristol Evening Post, I managed to get an exclusive interview with Sue Slocomb the manager of the victorious team. Both Sue and the team captain, Tammy Miller came from the Bristol area. Sue said, "For us to beat the USA on their own soil is something special. The US team are professionals and have been training here for a long time. They are used to the heat and humidity and I am really proud of the squad to have won under real pressure. They showed true grit, and now with this result we can get into the reckoning. In the first game we didn't play badly, but were beaten by a good Korean team. The second game against Holland we showed more grit to draw. After that I put on my hob-nailed boots and the girls really wanted to win, showing real character. We had great encouragement from the supporters"

Tammy Miller, the captain said, "I'm just relieved we played a lot better but it was hard", to which her mother Mary, who was standing beside her added, "It was a terrific victory. To defeat the USA, who were bronze medallists in the 1994 World Championships, was excellent. The Americans have been based as a squad here in Atlanta practising on this pitch for all of last year, and they know every bump on the pitch. It is great. The girls done good!"

Atlanta Olympic Games 1996

Wednesday 24th July

Stone Mountain Park lies about twenty miles north-east of Atlanta, and was the venue for the track cycling, tennis and archery competitions. On a glorious summer day, it is a very beautiful natural place; a noteworthy feature of the park mentioned in all the guide books is that it has the world's largest mass of exposed granite although this probably did not interest any of the highly focussed competitors a bit. Wherever you go in America they always like to have something that is the biggest in the world.

The Olympic Tennis Championship had been included in the first Olympiad held in Athens in 1896, but it was subsequently dropped. I had been given a couple of tickets for the cycling, and was able to swap one for the tennis event. It was far easier to get in to watch the Olympic Championships than to get hold of a ticket to Wimbledon.

The tennis competition taking place here in Stone Mountain Park, was in a truly delightful setting. The majority of seats around the centre court were unoccupied, and many spectators were sweltering and sheltering under umbrellas. This was hardly surprising as the temperature on the centre court was said to be a stifling 104 degrees. I was able to watch the Australian Phillipousis playing; he had a serve reputed to be a very powerful 120mph plus.

The major names of the tennis world like Pete Sampras and Boris Becker had decided to give the Olympics a miss. However Andre Agassi, who had won Wimbledon four years before in 1992, had agreed to take part, and subsequently he went on to win the gold medal in this event. Although we were watching the early rounds, the competition seemed a bit flat, and had none of the atmosphere of Wimbledon; maybe the heat was just too much for people to cope with.

There was an interesting story printed in the Atlanta Journal about the tennis tournament later in the week. A doubles match featuring the American pair Andre Agassi and MaliVai Washington had been scheduled for the 12,000 seat centre court. When the organisers announced that they were going to move it to Court Number One, fans who had waited through three hour rain delays took strong exception and created angry and noisy scenes. Thirty five police officers in full riot gear arrived at the scene. Can you imagine that at Wimbledon? Organisers sensibly decided to let the match remain on centre court.

Moving on to the cycling velodrome, I struck up a conversation with the man sitting next to me on the bus. It turned out that he was the manager of the Canadian track cyclist Curt Harnett, who was the current world record holder for the 1000 metre sprint; he had won the bronze medal in the 1992 Olympic Games in Barcelona. When we got to the stadium we found Curt sitting with his family waiting for his race. His manager introduced me to him.

He was powerfully built with long shoulder length wavy blond hair. They told me he regularly advertised leading brands of shampoo in Canada. Two little lads had t-shirts with 'Uncle Curt goin' for gold' printed in bold black ink on the back. Curt was photographed alongside one his male support team; in comparison his massive thigh muscles were about twice the size of those of his supporter.

The Velodrome track and surrounding structure reflected both the heat and light of the bright Atlanta sunshine, with the result that it was both dazzling and swelteringly hot. Standing at the top of the bends of the track, you looked down a steep slope of 42 degrees. Just looking was quite terrifying. The 1000 metre sprint is a tactical race between two cyclists. From the start the two cyclists move at snail's pace for about 800 metres as they manoeuvre for a good position. They try to avoid being forced into the front place, as there is some advantage in being in the slipstream of the leading rider; all the time they are eyeing each other waiting for a moment's weakness or lack in concentration. They slowly climb up the 42 degree banking and then one of them explodes down the slope into a frantic sprint over the last half of a lap. The first part of the race is just tactics, the second part is sheer brute speed. But it is always tremendously exciting.

Curt Harnett was beaten in his men's sprint semi-final by the American, Marty Northstein, who went on to win the silver medal. In the race to decide who would get the bronze medal, Curt beat the Australian Gary Neiwand to repeat his performance in Barcelona.

He retired after the games and is reputed to have said, "it is time to get a haircut and get a real job"'.

The Velodrome had been purpose built for the Olympics, and we were told that after the Games, it was to be dismantled and sold. I wonder what sort of market there was for a banked 400 metre Olympic velodrome track. One could imagine an advert along these lines 'for sale one used Olympic Games velodrome. Only one careful user'.

Atlanta Olympic Games
Thursday 25th July

The Judo finals were held at the Georgia World Congress Centre, which was a short walk away from the MARTA. On the way there was an almighty downpour; I found shelter for about twenty minutes till it stopped, and then the sun shone and everything was fine again. When it rains in Atlanta it really comes down in stair-rods, and this shower followed the usual pattern.

In the Judo arena there were two very colourful groups of supporters from Korea and Japan. The Japanese contingent were dressed uniformly in a smart yellow silk judo jacket, with a broad black ribbon edging round the front and collar and with a bold white Japanese inscription embroidered on it. On their heads they wore a white baseball cap with a red circle denoting the rising sun, and a further inscription in Japanese. On their backs were some more Japanese slogans and in English 'We love Tarumi' and 'Kobe, Japan', which I guess was their home town. There must have been at least a hundred of these uniformed supporters.

The Korean supporters were not dressed in the same uniform way, although many wore a yellow jacket, and a white tee-shirt with 'Korea' printed on the front. Although their dress was not as impressive as the Japanese support group, they outscored the Japanese from the noise aspect, as they all carried two long yellow lozenge shaped balloons, with 'victory Korea' and other patriotic slogans printed on the rubber. They banged the two balloons together in time, making a weird hollow sort of noise. Whether it was effective in encouraging their competitor I don't know, but while I was there they did not win a medal.

The finals took place on a large square mat, with a foot-wide red line marking the competition area. There was a referee, and at opposite corners two judges in suits were seated, holding coloured flags. They used these to denote the winner, if there was no definitive winner according to the scoreboard at the end of the bout.

The events taking place at that session were the finals of the 65kg division. The final was between Udo Quellmalz from Germany, and Yusimasa Nakamura from Japan. The result was a win for Quellmalz, who was so thrilled that he ripped off his judo jacket and danced around the mat in sheer uninhibited joy. It must have been a disappointment for the large body of dedicated Japanese supporters, to have to settle for the silver medal. There was no play-off for third place, so the losing semi-finalists Guimares of Brazil and Hernandez from Cuba, were both awarded a bronze medal.

The winners' rostrum was carried in and placed in the centre of the canvas square and the young girls marched in carrying the medals and a small bouquet of flowers on a tray. The medallists were announced and took their places on the rostrum. The medals were presented and with much emotion; the German national anthem was played, with the four flags raised slowly at the far end of the arena. Victory ceremonies are always a wonderful moment for the winner, but for every winner there have to be those that don't make it on the day.

I spoke to the father of the British competitor Julian Davies who told me, "After a bye, he beat his opponent Seck from Senegal with an arm lock in the second round. Unfortunately, he was beaten in the third round by Lewak of Poland, which was a big disappointment as he had beaten him four times before in the previous year. Julian had previously beaten both Quellmalz, and also the bronze medallist Hernandez of Cuba; unfortunately he didn't have a chance to repeat it, as he wasn't able to make it into the final rounds". His father went on to say that, to get to this level, it was necessary to train full time. He added that the Olympic Judo competition was extremely well organised and everybody was really friendly. He would have re-mortgaged the house to come to Atlanta; the atmosphere was terrific. They had not experienced any difficulties with the transport, which was an interesting comment as the press at that time were really having a go at the authorities over the delays encountered. Richard Hopkins of Devizes, a 4th dan performer said "I have trained with Julian for 18 years. Even though he was not successful here we still feel proud to be here to support him".

Another event taking place in the same venue was the ladies table tennis, or as the Americans like to call it 'ping-pong'. I was surprised how colourful it was. There were eight tables in the hall; all had a purple surface, contrasting with the pink floor. This was quite different to any table tennis I had ever seen played before where the tables traditionally were a bottle green. The competition ball was orange; I had only ever seen a white ball. There were three judges and a referee, at each table.

The players I saw were Huberta Vreisekoop of Holland and Ruta Garkauskaita of Lithuania. They were playing in a round-robin game in Group 'N'. It was a very vocal match with the player who won each point shouting excitedly to her supporters and shaking her fist triumphantly at her coach. Neither player subsequently seemed to progress any further than the round-robin stage, where all the players in a group play each other, and those with the best results move on.

An American girl, Amy Feng , playing in her round-robin match was being well beaten, but the home crowd raised the roof every time she managed to win a point. She would rush up to the net and wipe her hands on the top of the table, and with the customary response shake her fist at her coach. These were only the early rounds but, apart from the local supporters following her game, there were just a handful of people watching the other matches.

Walking through the town with another volunteer, we saw a man sitting alone on a seat wearing a T-shirt emblazoned with 'I'm Bob Hayes. 100 metre gold medallist'. We walked over to say hello and had a chat about the games. He also posed with us for a photo. Bob had won the 100 metres in the Tokyo Olympic Games 32 years earlier in 1964, equalling the world record in exactly 10 seconds.

After the Olympics, he became a professional football player with the Dallas Cowboys. During a nine year football career, he was a member of the team when they won the final of the Super Bowl, and was awarded the coveted ring that is presented to the winning team members. He was the only man on record to win an Olympic gold medal and the victory ring. His nick-name was 'The Bullet'.

Great as it had been to experience the other sports, I went back to my accommodation that night knowing that tomorrow the real Olympic competition begins, the athletics, or as the Americans like to call them the 'track and field' events.

Atlanta Olympic Games 1996

Friday 26th July

Today was the start of the athletics competition in the main stadium, and would be the first time the stadium volunteers had to work since the opening ceremony. As our team was on duty for the evening session, we were not required until 5.30 so I had a chance to watch the weight-lifting in the morning.

I had a particular interest in one weight-lifting event as the local paper had asked me to look out for Anthony Arthur from Bristol who was taking part in the 83kg category. In the snatch, he lifted 140kg and 147.5kg with ease. When he attempted the British record at 152.5kg, he managed to get the bar onto his chest but could not straighten his knees to get it above his head. His grandfather, who coached him, said that although he had been very tense before the competition, he had performed well and finished in 12th place. His aggregate of 327.5 kg in the snatch and clean and jerk was some way behind the winner Dimos Pyrros of Greece whose aggregate was 392kg.

I went on to the stadium to report for duty. The first day of the athletics events is not usually very exciting, with only a couple of low-key finals being competed for. There were two sessions in the stadium and they were watched by over 160,000 spectators. In the morning session the first round heats of the sprints were held. All the fastest men in the world were performing, although not necessarily against each other. In the first round of the 100 metres there were 12 heats with nine running lanes, and over 100 competitors to whittle down. The first three in each heat qualified, plus the four fastest losers. A total of 40 qualified for the next round, the quarter finals.

The first of the athletics finals that took place in the early part of the day was the 20 kilometre walk, which was won by Jefferson Perez of Ecuador. It is an event which rarely makes headlines, although in Ecuador that day it almost certainly would have done, as this was the first Olympic medal his country had ever won. He became a national hero, and on his return home he gave thanks for his victory at the cathedral in Quito, then walked the 450 kilometres to his home town in Cuenco. His fellow country-men turned out along the route to applaud him.

For the evening session, I had been allocated to the team with Bruce Freniere, our team leader. He had an impressive CV as a volunteer, having served at the Barcelona Olympics four years before. He had also worked at the Pan-American Games, which compares in scope with the European games. He had regularly attended the major national athletics meetings in the USA and his wife Peggy was also a volunteer heading up another team.

As a team leader, he was a great guy to work with as he was well known and trusted. Consequently he was assigned some pretty good places in the stadium. Our team was six to eight members-strong throughout the games. For this first night we were assigned to the section by the start of the 100 metres.

Although it could be argued that the shot put identifies the strongest man in the games, it generally takes place in a small obscure section in the centre of the track. The distances thrown are nowhere near as far as in the hammer, discus and javelin events. Many spectators sitting in the stands will be able to watch the trajectory of the javelin as it soars high in the air before plummeting into the grass 90 metres away. The shot normally lands in a pit and covers a little over 20 metres. The event just doesn't have the same spectator appeal nor the excitement.

It was the only final of the evening session and included some strong American competitors, so the home crowd were very pumped-up and noisy. With one round of throws still to go, Godina of USA, and del Soglio of Italy were leading, with the American, Randy Barnes, who was the favourite way back in sixth position. In the final round Barnes unleashed the best throw of the competition to win the gold convincingly by nearly a metre, in 21.62 metres. The home crowd went wild. They absolutely loved it, with great whoops of 'USA! USA!' This was the first track and field gold medal for the home supporters, and as the second place was taken by another American they revelled in the added bonus of the silver medal. The track and field programme had started well for the home supporters, and would continue to do so over the next week, with many medal ceremonies accompanied by the American national anthem. Barnes had been the silver medallist eight years before, in 1988 in the Seoul Olympic Games.

The rest of the evening programme was taken up with heats for sprints and the qualifying events for women's javelin and men's triple jump. Tessa Sanderson a former British Olympic gold medallist didn't manage to get through to the final in the javelin. Jonathan Edwards was regarded as a strong British medal hope for the triple jump and qualified for the final just a shade behind the leaders.

There were some top athletes competing in the quarter finals for the 100 metres and 400 metres for both men and women. In the 100 metres men's quarter-finals, there were two world class performances by Frankie Fredericks and Ato Bolden, who were recorded at 9.95 and 9.93 and who appeared to be easing up at the end. Any time faster than 10 seconds in a heat has to be pretty impressive. The holder of the Olympic title, Linford Christie of

Great Britain, came through his early rounds without any serious threat.

In the women's 100 metre event, Gail Devers, the defending champion went through the two early rounds with comparative ease. Not only is Gail a top world sprinter, but she has probably the longest finger nails of any athlete. They must be somewhere between three to four inches long and curl into a crescent shape. When starting a race a sprinter normally spreads their fingers behind the start line. Gail somehow clenches her fists so her fingers protect the nails from breaking as she bursts from the starting blocks.

In the 400 metre heats, there was an interesting finish to heat five. Michael Johnson, world record-holder, and unbeaten for so long, was regarded as the greatest certainty to win the gold medal. He eased down in the last few metres to be passed by an unknown Sri Lankan, Sugath Thilakaratne who dipped at the finish and just pipped the great man, finishing in 45.79, just one 100th of a second faster. The fairy story ended there as he later failed to make the final, but he achieved something few others could claim to have done, and that was to put Michael Johnson into second place. Still the objective of a heat is to qualify for the next round; Michael Johnson did just that. Roger Black gave Britain hope by winning his first heat.

The heats provide a lot of races to watch as they sort out the wheat from the chaff, but they tend to be high on quantity, lower on quality as many top performers want to save their best for later and settle for just qualifying. As the main requirement is to eliminate competitors, most of the interest is in which top names might fail to make it.

It had been quite a hard day for the volunteers, and after we had cleared through the stadium for any bombs or stragglers I took the MARTA and a couple of buses to get home. There was a good spirit among the travelling volunteers as we exchanged our 'war stories' and experiences to date.

Atlanta Olympic Games 1996

Saturday 27th July

I had returned home late, and had only been in bed a couple of hours when there was a knock on the door; Janice my landlady had come upstairs to tell me that there was a call from the Bristol Evening Post in England wanting to talk to me about the bomb! They had my telephone number as I had agreed to send them information about the progress of the West Country Olympic competitors.

Their duty night reporter in Bristol, Julie Welch, had picked up my name from the files and rang to ask if I had anything to say about the bomb blast. Of course having been fast asleep in bed I knew absolutely nothing, so I told her that I would find out what I could and phone her back.

Although it was about three a.m. there was still a 24 hour American television channel reporting the news as it came in and I made some notes from that. At first there had been bewilderment and shock. The initial TV reports indicated that there was a free rock-concert at the Olympic Centennial Park. The blast was believed to have come from behind the building being used by the Swiss watch manufacturer, Swatch. Shrapnel had been found as far as a block and a half away. People standing on a tower and some police had been injured by flying glass. There were pictures on TV of some policemen with blood running from cuts, receiving attention from the paramedics. Police were still trying to clear the area of people who had been attending the concert. At that stage it was believed there were four fatalities. I phoned back to the Bristol Evening Post and told Julie Welch what I had learned from the TV reports.

Later it was confirmed that one woman had been killed as a result of the bomb, and a Turkish press-man had died from a heart attack while running to the scene of the blast. Over 100 people were injured. Ironically, the group that had been performing on the stage at the time of the blast were called Jack Mack and Heart Attack. The police had received a warning earlier but, by the time it came in, it was too late to evacuate the park.

There was absolutely no doubt that the games would go on. President Clinton said, "An act of vicious terror like this is clearly directed at the spirit of our own democracy. We must not let attacks stop us from

75

going forward. We cannot let terror win. This is not the American way".

We learned later that the weapon was a pipe-bomb concealed in a knap-sack containing nails and screws.

To satisfy the politicians, the organisers and a concerned public, the police needed to be seen to be on top of the situation. Within a couple of days, they were able to make an arrest. A security guard who at first had been hailed as a hero for helping people hurt by the blast, was later arrested for questioning as a suspect. The authorities were comforted by the fact that someone, who might have been a culprit, had been found. So they let the games proceed as if nothing had happened. Several years later the true culprit was found, and confessed that he had been the bomber, so the wrong man was made a scapegoat.

I went to the photo shop to hand in a couple of films, and another customer, Charlie asked me some questions about being a volunteer and the duties involved. He offered to give me a lift into town and told me he had recently developed a new chemical preparation for growing really big sunflowers. An advantage of wearing the uniform is that people are willing to offer you a lift, when they might be otherwise reluctant to do so for a total stranger.

That evening our team of volunteers had drawn the short straw. Bruce, our normal leader was not on duty, and the team were assigned to another group. We were manning the entry to the stadium near to the first bend of the track. As a result of the bomb, there had been some tightening up on the security measures. Spectators had to pass through a heavily-manned security check-point, before passing the entry gate, where volunteers were checking tickets to enter the stadium. Big queues were building up at this entry gate. At first when we started to check the tickets, people were fumbling in their bags and wallets trying to find them, with the inevitable delays and frustration to those waiting behind. I was working with Big John, and we made life easier by simply going down the line and saying, "Please have your tickets ready for inspection." Amazing! We were able to handle all the punters at twice the speed of the other lines. Having sorted out our line we announced, "Express lane, just have your tickets ready", and people transferred from elsewhere to use our rapid service.

We had noticed that some of the girl volunteers in nearby lines were following the guide-line approach as set out in the training manual by saying "Good evening, my name is Cindy-Lou, and I want to welcome you to the Olympic Stadium. Is there anything I can do to make your visit more enjoyable?" which took up several seconds per ticket-holder. Multiplied 100 times it lead to long frustrated queues. Frankly who cares about the name of the volunteer at the gate, and the 'How can I make your visit more enjoyable?' is a no-brainer. You can help the ticket-holders simply by getting them through as fast as possible.

For some reason, the authorities had decided that they wanted all the torn-off ticket stubs counted, so we had the frustrating job of counting stubs while some events were taking place in the stadium. However after a while there was a rebellion on the part of some of the volunteers and we were released to go and watch the activities inside. Nobody ever explained the purpose of the stub counting, nor why it had been considered necessary. We were never asked to do it again.

The main events of the evening were the men's and women's 100 metre races, and the triple jump final. In the men's 100 metre race Linford Christie from Great Britain was the defending champion. He was probably unique in an Olympic sprint final in that he was a grandfather. In the earlier rounds, Frankie Fredericks, arguably Namibia's most famous citizen, and Ato Bolden from Trinidad had both run 9.93 seconds. Linford had finished third in his semi-final in over 10 seconds. However, British supporters hoped he had something up his sleeve for the final.

There were three false starts; first Linford Christie, and then Ato Bolden. At the third attempt Linford made his second false start and, as a result, was disqualified. He was not a happy bunny, and could be seen arguing with the officials, leaving the other seven competitors hanging around waiting for the race to start. The electronic starting device showed that Linford had false-started, and the track referee was called and indicated that he was out. He stripped his singlet from his shoulders and stood by the track, with his hands on hips, shaking his head in disgust.

At the fourth attempt the start was good, and what a race! Wearing the red, blue and green colours of

Namibia, Frankie Fredericks was just leading at about 60 metres, but then Donovan Bailey of Canada, in a white singlet and black shorts produced a phenomenal burst of speed in the last half of the race and won in a new world-record time of 9.84 seconds. Frankie Fredericks was second in 9.89 and Ato Bolden third in 9.90. The two American runners finished fourth and fifth, much to the despair of the home crowd. There had only been two previous Olympic Games, in 1976 (Montreal) and 1928 (Amsterdam) when American runners had failed to win a medal in the 100 metres.

In the women's 100 metre race, Gail Devers successfully defended her sprint title by winning the Olympic gold medal for the second time. The race was incredibly close with Devers and Merlene Ottey of Jamaica both being given the same time of 10.94 seconds. Photos of the finish show them very close together on the line, although Devers had bent her head forward to a greater extent than Ottey. The judges ruled that Devers had won by two centimetres. When Ottey appealed, she put forward the argument that it was the torso and not the head that had to cross the line first, but her appeal was refused. It does seem incredible that when times can be given to the precision of one hundredth of a second, athletes can be given the same time, and yet one is two centimetres ahead. Some people consider that in such a tight finish maybe a dead-heat could be given. It was particularly tough on Ottey as they had both been involved in a very close finish in 1993, when they shared the same time at the world championships. On that occasion the race had also been awarded to Gail Devers.

Gail Devers seemed to have a preference for the 100 metres hurdles, but had won back to back gold medals in the 100 metres sprint, and was only placed fourth in the hurdles final. Poor Merlene Ottey, she had performed at the Olympic Games in Moscow in 1980, Los Angeles in 1984, Seoul in 1988, Barcelona in 1992, and now in Atlanta. She had picked up silver and bronze medals in both sprints and also the relays, and to miss the gold by the thickness of a vest was absolutely devastating.

Britain had great expectations of a gold medal in the triple jump. In previous years, Jonathan Edwards had been the first man in the world to jump further than 18 metres and, at the time of the games, he held the world record at 18.29 metres. Furthermore he had been unbeaten for the last 22 competitions. Kenny Harrison from the USA, who had not been able to compete for a year through injury, led the qualifying round of the competition with a jump of 17.58 metres.

In the final, Harrison produced an excellent first jump of 17.99 metres. Jonathan Edwards started with two no-jumps. This was not good news for the British supporters and certainly not for Jonathan either because, if he didn't get the next one right, he could kiss goodbye to any medal hopes. However, in the true spirit of a star performer, his third jump got him into a medal position. In the final all competitors take three jumps, and the top six can take a further three jumps. Jonathan now had the chance to take three more jumps. He managed a respectable 17.88 in the fourth round, within just 11 centimetres of the leader.

Harrison took a break between jumps to cheer on his partner Gail Devers in the women's 100 metre race. He must have been inspired by her victory as he responded well with a leap of 18.09 to go into first place to win the title. It was a great disappointment for the British supporters as we had really hoped for our first track and field gold medal in this event.

There were two semi-finals of the women's 800 metres. In the first race, Kelly Holmes of Great Britain finished in third place to qualify for the final, to be run two days later.

This had been a 24 hours of astonishing contrasts. In the early hours, we had experienced the horrific incident of the bomb with the resulting fatalities and severe injuries. On the track, there had been two sessions- the morning and evening events- watched by over 150,000 spectators. The finals held in the evening all produced some magnificent performances, including the world record by Donovan Bailey and some very close finishes. The home crowd were happy with their two gold medals, and there were the emotional scenes at the playing of the Star Spangled Banner, the US national anthem, at the victory ceremonies. Sadly in the two events where the British supporters had high hopes of winning gold medals, Linford Christie was disqualified and Jonathan Edwards came second, so we had to be satisfied with a silver medal in the triple jump.

Congratulating Haile Gebrselassie of Ethiopia after his great victory in the men's 10,000 meters race.

I meet Bob Mathis the Decathlon gold medallist in 1948 and 1952.

Curt Harnett bronze medallist in the 1000 meter cycle
match sprint, with supporters.

The medals ready for presentation to winners of the men's
cycling road race.

Max Sciandri (Great Britain) who won the bronze medal in
the men's road race, leading Pascal Richard (Switzerland).

The pack follow the leaders in the women's cycling road
race.

The broom wagon ready to sweep up any stragglers in the cycle road race.

Two riders playing cat and mouse in the 1000 meters cycling event.

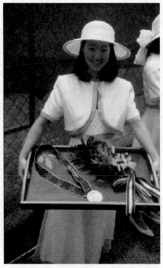

A gold medal ready for presentation.

Paola Pezzo (Italy) gold medallist in the women's mountain
bike cross country race.

Bart Brentjens (Holland) celebrates as he passes the jet-spray coolers in the approach to the finishing tape for the men's mountain bike cross-country race.

The victory ceremony for the women's cycle road race.

Japanese Judo supporters celebrate a silver medal.

Korean Judo supporters with their noisy balloons.

British hockey supporters. The sheik in his Union Jack outfit
in the bottom left of the picture

Mother of the goalkeeper of the Great Britain hockey team.

Supporters of Tim McRae celebrate his new USA record in the weight-lifting competition.

Supporters of 15 year-old Beth Botsford (USA) who won 100 meters backstroke.

Supporters of Tom Malchow (USA) silver medallist in the
men's 100 meter butterfly.

Family and friends of Michelle Smith celebrate her second
gold medal.

Richard Phelps (GB) in the Modern Pentathlon cross-country race.

The proud mother watches the final event in the
heptathlon as her daughter, Denise Lewis wins the bronze
medal.

Pole vault in action

Linford Christie

Thugwane of South Africa leads Bong Ju of Korea and Eric Wainana of Kenya into the stadium for the finish of the men's marathon. Sad to see the empty stands for the finish of an Olympic final event

Michael Johnson with a convincing lead in the 400 meters final.

This fire engine from Puerto Rico indicates how additional
resources to cope with the extra demands of the Olympic
Games were provided from far and wide

Bob Dole, the Presidential candidate mixes with the crowd.
(arrow points to Bob Dole ---------^ Dark suit)

Our team of volunteers stand on the gold medal podium
after the track finals are completed.

The Ticket office at a standstill while the computers are
fixed.

Atlanta Olympic Games

Sunday 28th July

The women's marathon race started at 7 o'clock to avoid the oppressive heat of the Atlanta daytime. I went to Lennox to watch the runners in the early stages of the race. Having watched the main bulk of the field go through, I caught the MARTA to a point just outside the stadium where the runners passed the 25 mile marker; they still had a mile and 385 yards to go. I stayed to watch the two British runners, both Scots, Liz McColgan and Karen MacLeod run past, but they were some way behind the leaders. Karen lived just outside Bristol. In the local press just before the event, she said she had prepared to go to hell and back, fearing both the heat and humidity. Some of her training included visits to the local swimming pool, running in water for hours in high humidity. The race was won by Fatuma Roba of Ethiopia, who finished two minutes ahead of Yegorova from Russia.

I arrived at the stadium early and had a chance to wander around before activities started. I went up to the third and fourth levels of seating. The third floor was mostly the hospitality suites, and the fourth level really should have had a health warning for those suffering from vertigo. It towered over the bends on the track below.

When the afternoon session started, Bruce's team were allocated the block right alongside the long jump pit, at ground level. This turned out to be an excellent location, and was the place where many of the British supporters were seated. Denise Lewis of Great Britain, was performing particularly well in the Heptathlon event, which had now entered its second day. The final event was the 800 metres, and Denise needed to finish well to win the bronze medal. Both her mother and coach were in seats in our block. As Denise was finishing the race I took a series of photos of her mother as she realised her daughter had scored enough points to win the bronze medal. Denise was a member of Birchfield Harriers in Birmingham, a club that I had belonged to about twenty years before and her coach was able to bring me up-to-date with the news of some of the club members I used to run with.

At one stage, Bruce asked me to stand by the entrance to the block of seats and make sure that only people with a valid ticket entered, even though there were quite a few seats unoccupied. A gentleman came up and asked if it would be OK for him to sit on one of the empty seats. In accordance with Bruce's instructions, I had to say politely that we could only allow entry to ticket holders with a seat in that block. He accepted this and walked away. Someone behind me said 'That was a great race you ran last night' and shook his hand. I realised later that it was the fastest man in the world I had prevented from taking a seat; he was Donovan Bailey winner of the 100 metres gold medal the night before!

We were well positioned to watch the men's hammer final, which was emotional and as well as dramatic. After the three preliminary throws, the first eight would qualify for a further three throws. Lance Deal of the USA was tied in eighth place with Sgrulletti of Italy both having thrown 76.94 metres. Normally in competition when this happens, the man with the best second throw would be ranked higher and, consequently, Deal would have been eliminated. However, as there was no precedent for such a tie-breaker to decide who can qualify for the additional throws, both athletes were allowed to qualify for the final.

The Hungarian Kiss was in the lead as they started the final round, throwing 81.24 metres, with Skvaruk second in 79.92. With his final throw Lance Deal, who was then in eighth place, unleashed a mighty throw of 81.12 metres, which took him into silver medal position, barely 12 centimetres short of the gold medal. The American crowd erupted and, in our block just in front of me, his family were celebrating. They were surprised and totally overjoyed, leaping up and down and waving their arms. Krykun of the Ukraine also produced a good final throw to take the bronze, leaving poor old Skvaruk dropping from second to fourth in the final round to miss out on the medals.

Shortly afterwards, Lance Deal came to our seating block with a big bunch of flowers. It was a very emotional scene, as he embraced his wife, and presented her with the flowers. When they realised who he was, everybody swarmed round him for a photograph, autograph or both. Amazing! One mighty throw to win silver and everyone wanted to know him. If he had finished eighth, no one would have bothered. On his way out, we shook his hand and congratulated him, I don't think that at that time the realisation of winning the medal had quite sunk in.

We were close to the high jump area, and it was a gripping final to watch. Javier Sotomayor of Cuba, was favoured by many to take the gold. Standing at 6ft 5 inches, he was the world-record holder and the first man to clear eight feet (2.44m). He had been unfortunate in his athletics career, as twice before Cuba had boycotted the Olympic Games, in 1984 in Los Angeles when many communist countries did not attend, and in 1988 when Cuba boycotted the Seoul games. He would have been an odds-on favourite to win at both Olympiads. He had won the gold medal in the 1992 games in Barcelona. In spite of an injured knee he qualified for the Atlanta final, but went out early in the competition only clearing one height and finished in 11th place.

If more than one athlete clears the same height, the judges look at the number of failures and attempts made at the lower heights. The three leaders- the

British jumper Steve Smith, Charles Austin of the USA, and Partyka from Poland- were playing a tactical game. Smith cleared 2.35 on his second attempt, although the other two cleared with their first jump. At 2.37, Partyka cleared at the second attempt, but Austin and Smith failed twice. If they had cleared that height at the third attempt, Partyka would have been higher placed at that stage, due to clearing with fewer failures. Smith and Austin had nothing to gain now by clearing 2.37 on the third attempt so they both passed on the third jump to try to clear a greater height. With the bar at 2.39, Partyka missed his first jump. Smith missed and was eliminated. Nevertheless, he won a great bronze medal for Great Britain. Austin had one jump left. If he failed Partyka would take the gold. He was the smallest man in the final, but produced a magnificent jump almost two feet higher than his own height and brought the home crowd to its feet amidst thunderous applause. This put him now in the gold medal place. Partyka had two more chances and opted to attempt a greater height, hoping to leap-frog back to in to the lead, but he failed and the Americans won yet another gold. Austin whose height is barely half an inch over six foot, took three more jumps in attempting to break the world record, which would also take him over eight feet, but he narrowly missed. Yet another gold medal for the American team. How the crowd loved it!

The favourite in the final of the women's 5000 metres was Sonia O'Sullivan from Ireland. She had won her heat comfortably and was the reigning world champion at this distance. However, the Chinese girl

Wang Junxia held world records in the 3,000 and 10,000 metres. Also in the field was Paula Radcliffe of Great Britain, who had not yet hit the headlines with her world- beating performances in the marathon. Wang had run in the 5000 metre heat two days before, and in the 10,000 heat one day before. Wang and Konga, a Kenyan broke away from the pack early on, and Paula Radcliffe spent much of the race making the pace for the pack of runners following about 30 metres behind. With a couple of laps to go, Wang went ahead of Konga, and won the gold medal in a new Olympic record. Paula stepped up the pace and at one stage looked as if she might win the bronze, but a couple of runners passed her in the last lap and, although she had run courageously, she finished outside the medals in fifth place. Konga became the first Kenyan woman to win an Olympic medal, surely the first of many.

The 5000 metres was a big disappointment for the Irish supporters who were all fired up after the triple gold medal success of their swimmer Michelle Smith and were hoping that some of the magic would inspire their runners to great performances. Sonia O'Sullivan, who was suffering from some sort of stomach upset, couldn't keep up and, with four laps to go, was dropping off the pace at the back of the field and looking very distressed. She dropped out with a couple of laps to go.

The media reported a bizarre incident before the qualifying heat a few days before that could well have affected Sonia. As the runners had taken off their track-suits to go onto the track, she was intercepted in the tunnel by an official and told she had to change her kit. She had to take off the outfit she was wearing because it displayed the wrong sports kit logo, and put on another with a different logo. There had been some dispute regarding the sponsorship of teams. Try to imagine the tension that competitors must experience during the moments just before an Olympic event, in front of 80,000 spectators and billions watching on TV. Now compound it by having to comply with some official telling her to strip off her kit and wear something else that had the approved logo. She was expected to do this in the tunnel where there were other athletes as well as a number of officials present

The days of amateur sport where taking part was more important than winning were long past. In Atlanta, it was all about corporate sponsorship, television schedules, drug testing and big bucks. Baron de Coubertin must have been turning in his grave.

There were two other notable events that afternoon: the qualifying round of the Men's Long Jump, and the semi-final of the men's 400 metres.

Michael Johnson of the USA had dominated the 400 metre event for several years and was current world champion, having won at both the last two world championships. He won his semi-final with consummate ease, looking casually over both shoulders for any possible threat in the final straight; he needn't have bothered; none of the others were anywhere near him. The home crowd roared their approval for another home success, albeit only a semi-final at this stage. For the Atlantan crowd, a win was a win regardless, and Michael Johnson was someone special. He took off both his spikes, which were appropriately gold, and threw them into the crowd.

Another Olympic mega-star, Carl Lewis, had a few traumas to cope with in qualifying for the long-jump final. He had won the event in 1984 in Los Angeles, 1988 in Seoul, and in 1992 in Barcelona. In the qualifying round, the top 12 competitors would go through to the finals the next day. With one jump still to be taken Carl Lewis, was down in 15th place, with a jump barely over 26 feet. We watched him sprinting down to the pit and he unleashed a jump of 27 feet 2.5 inches to register the longest jump of the qualifying round. He could easily have missed out on his fourth Olympic long jump final, but great champions always seem to find that extra something when they really need to.

In amongst all the competition events, there were the moving victory ceremonies. There was a great piece of music played as the medal winners came in for the ceremony. It was 'Bring on the Champions'. We saw two American victories- the high jump and the triple jump- which had been held over since Saturday. The home crowd let their feelings be known by their rapturous singing of the Star Spangled Banner. How I wished that Jonathan Edwards had been able to win the gold medal in the triple jump. The British track team had so far failed to win a gold. One of the strict rules for the volunteers was that you must not be seen to cheer any athlete, for fear of offending the supporters of another competitor. It would have been very hard not to wave the Union Flag, and sing the National Anthem had he won the gold.

The medal ceremony for the women's heptathlon was postponed until the following day, as one of the competitors was so emotionally overcome that she couldn't take part. They didn't tell us which one it was.

With so much going on in the stadium I really did not want to go away from the track in case I missed anything. Bruce came to me a couple of times to tell me it was my time to take a break. Volunteers were given a meal ticket which could be exchanged for food, but this meant going to the volunteer tent a little way away. Some days, I might give the food a miss. On others I would dash in to the tent and stuff a few bits and pieces into my pocket, get back to the track and surreptitiously grab a small mouthful at a time. We could always enjoy a drink kindly provided at one of the Coca Cola vending machines.

Last job of the day was always to sweep through the stadium looking for lost property, people hiding or suspicious looking objects.

After a really hard day at the stadium, followed by MARTA and bus trips, I got back to the house and found that I had forgotten my key. I rang the bell and banged hard on the door several times but no one answered. I went round the back of the house and banged hard on the back door and still no one responded. After half an hour of mounting anger and frustration I heard a group approaching, and it turned out to be a group of Dutch sports followers who were staying in the house for a few days, and they were able to let me in.

Atlanta Olympic Games
Monday 29th July

This was a fantastic night of superb performances. There was Michael Johnson winning the 400 metres nearly eight metres ahead of the British runner Roger Black, in a new Olympic record time. He had been unlucky in Barcelona in 1992 when he had been the favourite to win, but had food poisoning and failed to make the final. Never-the-less, he had won a gold medal in the 4 x 400 metre relay. He made up for it this time, having come through the earlier rounds, posting the fastest times and winning comfortably.

In the final, wearing gold spikes, he stormed to a blistering win, nearly a second ahead of his rivals, and easily the most convincing win in this event in the history of the Olympics. There were really two races- Michael Johnson way, way ahead - and Roger Black leading the other race, followed by ordinary mortals. It was good to see Roger win a silver medal, as he has had his share of injuries in the past. The third man to finish was Davis Kamoga from Uganda, who was something of a surprise finisher; while in fifth place was another British runner, Iwan Thomas.

Roger Black was quoted as saying, 'The only way to beat Michael Johnson is if he makes a mistake, and he doesn't make them. I was running for the silver medal tonight. For me, when Michael is running, the silver medal is my gold medal'.

Carl Lewis had won the last three Olympic long-jump gold medals. He had only just made the team in the US Olympic team trials, where he had finished third; rightly or wrongly, their selectors always pick the first three in each event at the trials, regardless of injuries or any other reason. Lewis had suffered from a lot of illness and injuries since the last Olympiad. His appearance at the final on this night was the result of his phenomenal final jump, which had taken him from 15th to first place in the qualifying competition the day before.

He did not start well, running through the pit to register a no-jump. His second jump was poor, but on the third he unleashed the jump that was to prove the winner at 8.50 metres. Mike Powell of the USA was the current world-record holder, but his best jump was some way behind at 8.17 metres. He seemed to be limping badly and there was a dramatic moment when, in a desperate attempt to find something for his final jump, Powell landed in the pit and fell forward on his face. The big display screens showed a grotesque image of him sadly getting up with his face and front of his body completely covered in sand. A sad ending for the man who, a few years before had beaten the incredible world record of over 29 feet set by Bob Beamon in the Mexico Olympics in 1968, which had stood for many years.

In winning his fourth gold medal in the long jump, Carl Lewis matched the performance of Al Oerter of the USA, who had won four gold medals in the discus, in successive Olympics. Al Oerter was the athlete who had brought the Olympic torch into the stadium the previous week, before handing over to Evander Holyfield. The winning jump by Carl Lewis was shorter than any of his previous gold medal- winning jumps.

For most athletes, to win a gold medal is the fulfilment of a life's ambition. Carl Lewis had just won his ninth, a truly staggering achievement.

There was another gold medal for the USA when Allan Johnson won the 110 metres hurdles. He appeared to knock down most of the hurdles, but never-the-less established a new Olympic record of 12.95 seconds. Colin Jackson of Great Britain, the world record holder, finished fourth, missing a medal by two hundredths of a second.

The women's 800 metres final featured Kelly Holmes of Great Britain, who was at the time a sergeant in the British Army. She was also a Judo champion. The two favourites were Mutola, a former football player from Mozambique, who had won the event in the World Championships in 1993, and Ana Quirot from Cuba. Masterkova from Russia took the lead early on and held on to beat the two favourites. Quirot came second and Mutola third, winning the bronze medal, the first ever Olympic medallist from Mozambique. Kelly Holmes took fourth place just one tenth of a second behind Mutola.

Sally Gunnell of Great Britain had won the gold medal for the women's 400 metre hurdles in Barcelona four years previously when she overtook the American Sandra Farmer-Patrick over the last few hurdles. Both of them were running here in the same semi-final race and the British supporters had great hopes that Sally would qualify for the final so she could defend her title later in the week. Sadly, these hopes were dashed in the second semi-final when Sally was unable to finish due to injury. Sandra Farmer-Patrick also failed reach the final by one 100th of a second. It was particularly sad for Sally as that day was her 30th birthday.

Ethiopia and Kenya have produced some of the finest runners in the world, where they live and train at high altitudes. The higher the altitude, the thinner the air, and that means less oxygen. The human body adapts to generate more red blood cells to circulate the oxygen more efficiently. This physiological adaptation is of great benefit to the distance runner used to living at higher altitude. Many runners used to living nearer sea-level spend time at high altitude training camps as part of their preparation for major events

There was another wonderful race; the men's 10,000 metres, probably the most thrilling event of the evening. There is always intense rivalry whenever Ethiopians and Kenyans meet in any race. Haile Gebrselassie of Ethiopia was the world-record holder for both the 5000 metres and the 10,000 metres, and was the holder of the world 10,000 metres title. He was generally regarded as the favourite to win. However there were three strong Kenyan runners; Paul Tergat, Paul Koech and Josphat Machuka. The first half of the race was run in 13 minutes 55 seconds, with a large number of runners in the pack, but around the halfway mark Koech and Machuka started to step up the pace and the leading pack was whittled down to six runners, including Haile and Tergat. With around five laps to go, Tergat put in a very fast couple of laps, and Gebrselassie followed closely behind. At this stage, the two leaders were going incredibly fast for a race of this distance and pulling away from the rest of the field. At the bell, Gebrselassie sprinted away and had opened up a gap of about 10 metres. Tergat tried to close it, but Gebrselassie won the gold in a new Olympic record of 27minutes 7.34 seconds. What was absolutely staggering was that the second 5000 metres of the race was run in a time that would have won all but two of the 5000 metre races run in Olympic history.

Haile Gebrselassie always seemed to be smiling, even when he must have been be suffering agonies in the last stages of the race. At the end of the race his feet were bleeding so badly from blisters, that he was forced to withdraw from the 5000 metre race to be run later in the week.

Shortly after the race, I was walking near the finish with John, one of the other volunteers, and we saw Haile standing nearby. We went over and congratulated him on his great win, and I asked if we could take a photo of me shaking his hand. He very kindly agreed, and John took the photo. He is only 5ft 4 inches and one of 10 children, but what a fantastic runner, and such a nice smiling friendly man. I have the photo framed and proudly hanging on the wall.

It had been a great evening for the home crowd; three gold medals, and their national anthem was played three times. For the British supporters, there were two fourth places, Kelly Holmes missing a medal by a 10th of a second, and Colin Jackson by two 100ths- so near and yet so far.

Atlanta Olympic Games
Tuesday 30th July

As there was no track and field programme at the main stadium planned for this day I was off duty. It seemed a good opportunity to go and watch the mountain bike racing. The Olympic Games had traditionally held the track and road cycling races in the scheduled programme, but mountain bike racing was introduced for the first time at the Atlanta Games. The course covered a distance of 47.7 kms, with some rocky surfaces and winding hilly woodland paths.

I arrived at the course in the Georgia International Horse Park, in time to watch the later stages of the men's race. It was so swelteringly hot, well into the 90s, that the organisers had set up a large fan arrangement alongside part of the route, with very fine jets blowing out a welcome spray to help the riders to cool off. The race was won quite easily by

Bart Brentjens, a florist from Holland. He was over two minutes in front of a Swiss rider, Thomas Frischknecht, the silver medallist. In third place was a Frenchman Martinez, an under 23 world champion who celebrated his medal when he finished by doing a 'wheelie', cycling with his front wheel lifted right off the ground.

By competing in a sleeveless top, Frischknecht, had failed to observe the proper dress code and was fined $5000. However, he was allowed to keep the medal. Curious that a mountain bike race should be won so convincingly by a man from Holland where there isn't a mountain in sight, over a Swiss where the country is full of mountains.

Between events, it was nice to be able to walk along part of the course which wound its way up and down a series of loops through woodland where it was relatively cooler. I found a good place to watch at the top of one of the tough little hills. The riders had to stand up, off the saddles to climb this hill. The winner of the women's race was an extremely attractive Italian girl Paola Pezzo, who had recently appeared in the glamour pages of various magazines. She was riding strongly at the front of the field with her cycling shirt unzipped to the waist, which was understandable in view of the stifling heat. It caused great excitement amongst all the male followers of mountain biking, and the photographers had a field day.

Approaching the finish, Paola raised both arms in triumph, and on crossing the line, promptly zipped up her shirt. When she got off her bike she seemed to be limping heavily as she went to greet her supporters. Alison Sydor of Canada, who was world champion, finished about a minute behind and to the joy of the American supporters Susan de Mattei was a surprise winner of the bronze medal.

If poor old Frischknecht was fined five grand for showing off his biceps, what price for Paola for showing far more parts of her well-endowed anatomy? Nevertheless she was without doubt a magnificent mountain cyclist and having won the gold medal in Atlanta, she went on repeat the performance by winning the mountain cycling event in the following Olympiad in Sydney in 2002.

From mountain biking, I made my way to the equestrian centre to watch the modern pentathlon event. On the walk there, I started chatting to a couple of people, one of whom turned out to be Brough Scott, who was covering the riding event for the Daily Telegraph. We walked together as far as the press box, at which point my accreditation badge would not allow further progress, but I was able to get a seat in the stand.

The idea behind the modern pentathlon was thought up by Baron Pierre de Coubertin, founder of the modern Olympic Games. A cavalry soldier behind enemy lines is sent to deliver a message. He sets off on an unfamiliar horse, but en route has to fight a duel using his sword. He escapes but has to shoot his way out of trouble with a pistol. He swims across a river, and finishes his task by running through the woods.

The Olympic events do not appear to follow this sequence.

At this stage, the modern pentathlon competitors had completed three of the disciplines; the shooting, fencing and 200 metres swimming race.

The fourth discipline was the riding event. Each competitor was paired with a horse for the very first time only 20 minutes before the start, which didn't allow much time to learn about any idiosyncrasies the horse might have before going round the jumping ring. The British competitor, Richard Phelps, excelled himself by doing a splendid clear round, gaining 1100 points. He was one of only three competitors to manage this. The man sitting next to me turned out to be his uncle, Robert Phelps, a former Olympic modern pentathlon competitor who coached him. Robert said, "It was a very tough field, and finishing in 18th place overall, he had put some very good people behind him. He swam well, he rode well but his shooting let him down. He had suffered from a virus and injured his Achilles tendon during the build up to the games". He was very complimentary about the British Olympic Committee, who had provided excellent facilities for the athletes in Tallahassee in the build-up prior to the games.

There had been some talk about dropping the modern pentathlon from the Olympics. In earlier Olympiads, the event had been held over four or five days. They had decided instead to run all the five disciplines of the event in one day for the first time. The competition had started about 7 am and, by the time the final event was completed the competitors had been going for well over 12 hours. This was further complicated by the fact that the earlier events had taken place at another location nearly 40 miles away, and there were some problems with the transport between the venues.

The final event was the 3km run, where they started at different times with handicaps based on their performances in the four other disciplines. The leader at that point was the Italian Toraldo, who started first, to be followed 15 seconds later by Parygin of Kazakhstan, and Zenovka of Russia after another 45 seconds.

For the spectator, the formula was simple; the finishing sequence in this handicapped race determined who won the gold, silver and bronze medals; first past the post in the run would be the winner. Toraldo was soon overtaken, leaving Parygin and Zenovka to battle it out to the finish. A few yards from the finishing line, Zenovka fell, and Parygin passed him to take the gold. Zenovka struggled to his feet just in time to take the silver.

On the track, the men's decathlon and the women's heptathlon take place over two days. The final event is a race where the competitors all line up on the start-line and, when the gun is fired, they all start together. At the end of the race, points are awarded depending on the times of each individual competitor, and there is a mathematical calculation necessary to determine who has won. One competitor may have to beat another by a time such as 6.7

118

seconds to win. No one knows the result until the compilations have been completed. The way this modern pentathlon final race was run was, without doubt, far more spectator-friendly. At the start of the final running event, the point's differential from the four previous events had been converted into times, and the starting times of the competitors were staggered accordingly. The man who had accumulated the most points to date started first and how soon the others could start depended on how far behind they were at that stage.

Talking to some spectators, it appeared that there was no transport provided for them between the modern pentathlon venue where the earlier events had taken place and the International Horse Park; access was further hampered by road-blocks. For those who had tried to watch all five events, quite a lot of leg work in sweltering heat had been necessary. The feeling amongst some of the spectators was that it was a great pity that there was not a better level of transport for people who had paid out a lot of money for an 'event ticket'.

Reaching home quite late after a busy day, I tried to open the front door. I had remembered the key this time. The problem was that Janice had gone to bed early and left her brother, who was staying for a few days, to lock up. He had put the bolts across inside the door and gone to bed himself. I was not very pleased. Fortunately he heard me ringing and bashing hard on the door and was able to let me in.

Atlanta Olympic Games

Wednesday 31st July

As I was not required for duty at the stadium until the evening, I went to watch the men's cycling road race. The race was 137.7 miles long and started quite close by at Buckhead at 8.30am and took just under five hours to complete. It was one of the few Olympic events where viewing was absolutely free of charge. When I reached the side of the course, the crowds were about 10 deep, and straining to get a view was quite difficult. Moving around, I found a place on the other side of the road where it wasn't crowded and there was a perfect uninterrupted view.

Among the starters was the American Lance Armstrong. The home country fancied his chances for a medal, although a few weeks earlier he had dropped out of the Tour de France after only five days, with bronchitis. In this road race, he finished in 12th place. He also competed in the Olympic time trial event where he finished sixth. These two performances were quite astonishing as in the next couple of months his health deteriorated and, in October, he was diagnosed with testicular cancer. It is well known that he received successful treatment and, when he had recovered, he went on to win the Tour de France an unprecedented seven times. A few other great cyclists had won the Tour five times in succession, but Lance was something special.

Three riders had broken away with about 20 miles to go; Sorenson, a Dane, Pascal Richard, a Swiss and Maximilian Sciandri of Great Britain. Sciandri took the lead at one stage a few hundred yards from the finish, but was overtaken with a couple of hundred yards to go, and eventually finished third. Richard of Switzerland won, with Sorensen of Denmark second. The winning time was 4 hours 53 minutes 56 seconds but only two seconds separated the first three. Max Sciandri is an Anglo-Italian who was born in Derby. He was no mean performer and, in 1995, had won a stage in the Tour de France.

I saw three girls holding the trays with the winning medals just prior to the medal ceremony. They let me take a close-up photograph of the gold medal; the closest that I got to any medal. Shortly afterwards, the three medallists passed by and I said congratulations to Max Sciandri. I can only describe his reaction as an angry scowl. He did not look particularly happy.

There was a rumour that Sorenson celebrated his silver medal that night by dancing on a table in a night club, wearing his medal around his neck and not much else.

On reaching the stadium for duty, I found that Bruce's team had been allocated the area alongside the finishing line, an absolutely superb spot to watch the track events. I was working in front of the British TV commentary box and had a chance to talk to Brendan Foster and Steve Cram. At that stage, there had not been too much to get excited about in the performance of the British athletes. The Olympic sprint champion Linford Christie had been disqualified in the final, and another big hope Colin Jackson, who held the world record for the 110 metres hurdles, had finished outside the medals in fourth place, in this his third Olympic final.

There were good facilities at the stadium for spectators in wheelchairs. Kim, one of the girls I had met at a training session, had the responsibility for accompanying wheelchair ticket holders to their places. I talked to one man in a wheelchair who told me that, in 1941, he had run within two tenths of a second of the 880 yards world record, and was then called up to fight in World War II. In those days, it was normal to run races over distances measured in yards and miles. He asked if I could find an old friend of his, Herb McKenley, who was manager of the Jamaican team. Herb had a superb Olympic record, having won silver medals in the 400 metres in 1948 and 1952, as well as holding the world record. He had said that he entered the 100 metres really 'to practise his starting' and finished with a silver medal. Just for good measure, he was part of the Jamaican 4 X 400 metre relay team that won the gold medal in 1952 in world-record time. It was a pleasure to go and find such a fine athlete and lead him to his old friend; they chatted together for about half an hour.

The men's decathlon is held over two days, with five events on each. This was the first day and the runaway favourite was the American world-record holder, Dan O'Brien. He had beaten the record set by Britain's double- gold medallist Daley Thompson three years before. His large family and support team were sitting in our section and the Americans were very vociferous in their support. He had been a strong favourite to win in 1992 in Barcelona but had failed to record a score in the pole vault in the US trials and consequently did not make the American team. In Atlanta, he made no mistake taking the lead after the third event, the shot put, and following that by doing well in the high jump and 400 metres. At the end of day one he was well in the lead.

In the 100 metre hurdles, Gail Devers was the big local favourite, having won the 100 metre gold medal in both the Barcelona and Atlanta events. Devers had won the World Championship 100 metres hurdles and clearly regarded it as her best event. However, she finished outside the medals in fourth place. The winner was Ludmila Engquist, now representing Sweden but who had previously competed for the USSR in Seoul in 1988. She had married her manager and went to live with him in Sweden. She was granted Swedish nationality barely a few weeks before the games. The race between her and the Slovakian Bukovec was neck and neck all the way, with only one 100th of a second separating the gold and silver medals.

The two steeplechase semi-finals were run with the first seven runners in each race to qualify. In one race after the first few laps, a group of seven runners had sorted themselves out in the front of the field. The wiser heads recognised that they had only to keep going at a modest pace to qualify for the final a couple of days later. They were all trotting along, gently conserving their energy, when a tattooed American athlete, Marc Davis, burst to the front. The crowd, realising that an American was in the lead, roared him on, and he reacted by sprinting as fast as he could over the last couple of laps. None of the other runners responded, and the leader charged into the home straight waving to his supporters in triumph as if he was about to win a gold medal. The day had not been a good one for the home crowd; some of their favourites had failed to win gold. Here was an American 'winner'; it was his moment of glory, and they raised the roof for him. Winning this heat was really meaningless. He would still have qualified for the final if he had finished seventh and would have saved a lot of energy. In the steeplechase final, two days later, he did not feature at all; no doubt all his energy had been burnt up in the semi-final.

The final of the 800 metres was a thriller. There had been three semi-finals with the first two finishers to qualify, plus the fastest losers. The Norwegian Rodal finished third in his heat and only qualified as the fastest loser. Johnny Gray of the USA, who had competed in three 800 metre Olympic finals before this, charged into the lead. Rodal and Sepeng were at the back of the field early in the second lap. Gray was still in the lead at about 600 metres, but then Rodal passed him on the final bend and held on to win. He became the first Norwegian runner ever to win a gold medal. Sepeng overtook several runners in the finishing straight to take the silver and became the first black South African athlete ever to win a medal.

Most of the medals so far had gone to the USA and other major athletics powers. It was wonderful to see a gold medal go to a smaller country like Norway. The Rodal story was particularly inspiring. His home was in Trondheim, in Northern Norway, where the winters they experienced were exceedingly harsh and the hours of darkness very long. Rodal had to do his winter training in a tunnel, about 300 metres long.

Atlanta Olympic Games

Thursday 1ˢᵗ August.

We had been told to report early that day, so Peggy and Bruce, the leader of our group picked me up from my digs. It was very good of them to do this as it saved a 20 minute walk, a bus ride, a train ride and a lengthy walk to get to the stadium. I found that working a long stint at the stadium, and then having to do the return journey made an exhausting day. There was generally very little opportunity to sit down in the stadium. If you went to sit down in the volunteers' meal tent, you would run the risk of missing something.

Bruce's team were allocated a place alongside the start line for the sprint events. The sun was shining brightly and it was very hot in the stadium. Nothing much was due to happen until 5 o'clock, so there was really no need for us to be there so early, but it gave us the chance to wander round the stadium chatting, to the athletes, coaches and celebrities.

The only competition of any real significance during the afternoon was the second day events of the decathlon competition. I watched the pole vault, as we were close by. I talked to the man standing next me, who was Harry Dost, the pole-vault and decathlon coach for Holland. He pointed out some interesting aspects of different techniques.

The Olympic Games and the American Presidential elections always take place every four years and coincide in the same year. In 1996, President Clinton was enjoying a very high profile in Atlanta, having played his part at the opening ceremony and visiting the athletes in the various stadia and the Olympic village. His opponent, the Presidential candidate Bob Dole, had no role to play and was right off the radar. In an attempt to get a share of the action, he decided to turn up one afternoon to be seen around and to shake a few hands, or 'press flesh' as the media liked to call it. He had a ticket in our block and, as soon as he took his seat and was recognised, there was a rush from the nearby spectators to shake his hand and get a photo.

His arrival seemed to cause great consternation amongst the security men, who appeared to have been taken completely surprise. Clinton had been seated in the VIP area, which could be policed easily, but Bob Dole had deliberately placed himself in the open public seats. Frantic security men were walking up and down the aisles, muttering into their mobile phones, but apparently helpless to do anything about it. He stayed a couple of hours before leaving. In the Presidential election three months later in November, he lost to Bill Clinton.

Another celebrity who was watching the events was Bob Mathias of the USA. At the London Olympics in 1948, Bob was only a seventeen-year-old. His coach had persuaded him to take up the decathlon just three months before the US trials, and he qualified for the US team. He went to Wembley and won the gold medal. The final event was the 1500 metres which didn't finish until 10.30 in the evening, in the gathering gloom. This was in the days before we had floodlights in the stadium. It was a magnificent performance for such a young athlete to win a multi-discipline technical event.

In the Helsinki Games in 1952 he repeated his performance winning by the largest margin in this Olympic event. He later served in the US Congress for four years. He was easy to recognise, plastered across the back of his t-shirt was ' I'm Bob Mathias'. I went to have a chat with him and had a photograph taken shaking his hand. He was very friendly and willing to chat about the games, athletics and his Olympic achievements.

When the evening session started, we showed people to their seats and, after a very short time there was a tremendous thunderstorm. There was no cover over the seating area, so everybody rushed for the shelter behind the stand. Naturally, when they all returned, their seats were soaking wet. I spent the next half hour or so dispensing paper hand-towels to dry the seats. Just think; I had come all the way to Atlanta to act as a human paper- roll-holder.

When the events got under way, there was plenty for the home crowd to get excited about. Running in the final of the 400 metre hurdles was Derrick Adkins, who was an engineering graduate from the local Georgia Tech, having lived in Atlanta for some years. He ran really well in front of an ecstatic home crowd and won the race from Samuel Matete of Zambia, who had been an old rival for some years. They had competed against each other many times. After the race Adkins said, 'I feel like I don't have to win another race in my life'.

It is always quite emotional, watching powerfully-built Decathlon competitors running the 1500 metre race. They have given their all in competing over nine challenging events in the past two days and, as a finale, they have to race over three and three quarter laps of the track in the 1500 metres. Decathletes don't have the light physique of the middle distance runners, and to have to run this sort of distance is mentally and physically very demanding. To try to get some perspective, the Olympic men's 1500 was won in 3minutes 35seconds, and the women's 1500 metres was run in a time just a shade over 4 minutes. The first eight competitors in the Decathlon 1500 metres ran times between 4.30 and 4.46. Dan O'Brien time was the slowest of the first eight in 4.45.8. If he had run that time in the final of men's 1500 metre race, he would have been lapped!

However in the decathlon Dan O'Brien went into the last event with a lead of over 200 points, accumulated over the first nine events, which meant that he did not have to win the race, but had to finish within 32 seconds of the second- placed man, Frank Busemann of Germany. This he did comfortably, in a time only 14 seconds behind, to win the decathlon gold medal, to the great joy of the home spectators, happy to cheer another American winner.

The women's 200 metres was due to be run 15 minutes before the men's 200 metres. The French runner Marie-Jose Perec had already won the 400 metre race a couple of days before and was attempting the same double as Michael Johnson. The two main contenders in the race were Perec who had won her semi-final heat, and Merlene Ottey who had won the other. Merlene had an incredible record in this event having won the bronze medal in Moscow (1980), Los Angeles (1984), Barcelona (1992) and she had finished fourth in !988 in Seoul. She was the first athlete to qualify five consecutive times for the final in the same event. A couple of days earlier, she had finished second in the 100 metres with the same time as the winner Gail Devers.

Ottey was the early leader in the final, but Perec caught her just before the finishing line and won by about a metre. In doing so, she completed an incredible 200 and 400 metre double. This threw the American supporters into confusion because 10 minutes later Michael Johnson, who had already won the men's 400 earlier in the week, was running the 200 metres to attempt his incredible double. Perec had pre-empted the great man by completing hers first.

The most spectacular performance of the day was in the 200 metres. Everybody regarded Michael Johnson as a cast iron certainty to win both 200 and 400 metres. It must be a great burden to carry that weight of expectation into an Olympic final, knowing that probably 2 billion people will be watching worldwide. When the first programme schedule had been published by the IAAF, the semi-finals of the 200 metres were due to be run on the same day as the 400-metre final. It was said that an appeal had been made to the programme organisers to change the programme so the 400-metre event could be completed before the 200 heats started. They agreed to the change after some hesitation, so that the double could be attempted

There had been much speculation in the press about whether he would be wearing gold spikes. He certainly did but he was moving so fast you could hardly tell. The atmosphere in the stadium was electric at the start and, just after the gun fired, he appeared to stumble ever so slightly and then simply tore away from the rest of the field. His very distinctive style of running, with his great barrel chest pushed out and a very straight-back, was in a different league from all the other finalists. He beat the second runner Frankie Fredericks by about four metres in a time of 19.32 seconds breaking the world record by 0 .34 seconds. In fact, Frankie Fredericks also only just missed beating the world record time by 200ths of a second, and achieved the third fastest time ever. There was a moment of disbelief as the finishing time was shown on the board, then the crowd roar was deafening. When Johnson saw his time, he threw up his arms in celebration, and then pulled on the straps of his USA singlet to show the world he was number one and this was his country. He did a lap of honour with an ice pack wrapped round his ham string; apparently it had given him a slight twinge in the latter stages of the race. He had achieved the incredible 200 and 400-metre double.

There was some interesting speculation in the American press; should the winner of the 100 metres be recognised automatically as the fastest man in the world? Some say the answer is obvious, but an American point of view was that Michael Johnson was actually the fastest man in the world. The world-record time of Donovan Bailey in winning the 100 metres final was 9.84 seconds, Johnson's time for exactly twice the distance of 200 metres was 19.32 seconds, giving an average per 100 metres of 9.66 seconds, therefore faster. Arguments between different camps of athletics geeks about whether the second part of the 200 metres included a flying start were put forward without any resolution.

An enterprising promoter, seeing a great money-spinning opportunity to try to settle the issue, organised a race the following year in Toronto. It was to be over 150 yards and, to make it fair, included a bit of bend and a bit of straight.

The race turned out to be a rather damp squib. Bailey got a good start and seemed to be pulling away around 100 yards, when Johnson pulled up with an injury, clutching his quadriceps. Bailey went on to win in 14.99 seconds, and picked up the prize of 1.5 million dollars.

There was another gold medal event that took place on this day, although at a different venue. Women's soccer was being held for the first time ever at these Olympic Games, and the gold medal was won by the American team. They beat China in the final by 2-1, in front of a crowd of 76.000 jubilant spectators, who gave them a standing ovation at the end. The *Atlanta Journal* said that an American team member had promised that, if her team won she would run naked through the streets. They did, and she did. She waited until 2.00 am, and then ran about 10 yards down a side street, wearing only her medal.

Sadly I missed both of these events.

The home of baseball is undoubtedly the USA, so it was a big disappointment that the home team was well and truly beaten by the Japanese team 11-2 in the semi-final. The Japanese went on to lose to Cuba in the final. After the jubilation of the home crowds when supporting their home teams, there was a certain smug satisfaction among the visiting sports supporters when this result was announced.

Atlanta Olympic Games
Friday 2nd August

In the morning I went to the Omni Coliseum where the indoor volley ball was taking place. This was a magnificent arena for the event. Although the tickets were supposed to have been sold out, I managed to buy one outside from someone at less than normal price. When I got in, I was surprised to find that the hall was only about 10% full. How come they were sold out? However, it was nice to have the opportunity to be able to move around freely to find the seats with the best view.

The game was between Argentina and Bulgaria. Both sides had tall men in the team and with Olympic glory at stake, it was thrilling to see the 100% commitment as these big men threw themselves across the courts, sliding on their fronts in their efforts to get a finger-tip to the ball before it hit the ground. It was an exciting match; best of five games. Bulgaria won the first two games; then Argentina came back to win the next two to make it two-all. In the deciding game it was neck and neck up to 15-15. Argentina went on to win 20-18. In the end, the result did not have any bearing on the medal positions as this was a play-off for the teams that finished seventh and eighth in the competition.

During each interval in the volleyball games, two smartly-dressed squads consisting of three sweepers marched onto the court with military precision and then proceeded to sweep and polish the floor, mopping up any droplets of sweat from the hot players. They were very well drilled, sweeping in time together, and completed the operation very quickly and slickly.

While this cleaning operation was taking place, the song 'YMCA' was played and a song leader encouraged the audience to join in singing and miming the actions of YMCA with their arms. The spectators responded with great gusto and enthusiasm. I find the introduction of a cheer-leader or song-leader adds a great deal of enjoyment to an event, and I wonder why we don't do more of it in Britain.

I had never watched indoor volleyball before, and was surprised to find that the game could be so exciting, even though the result was of little significance. Everyone had said how great the ladies beach volley ball was, with magnificent Brazilian and Australian beauties competing. Unfortunately, I didn't get the chance to watch it.

I moved on to the stadium where there were several track and field finals that afternoon. In the women's long jump, the home supporters had great expectations for Jackie Joyner-Kersie who over the last two Olympics, had amassed five medals. Earlier in the week she had injured her hamstring and was forced to withdraw from defending the heptathlon that she had won in Barcelona. Due to the injury, she had not performed to her usual high standard and, when she lined up to take her final jump she was lying seventh. In spite of the strapping covering most of her knee and thigh, she produced a fine leap to take the bronze medal, by barely an inch.

The unexpected winner of this long jump competition was Chioma Ajunwa, a policewoman from Nigeria. She became the first African ever to win an Olympic gold medal in a field event. Looking very smart in the green and white singlet of Nigeria, she seemed to be tiny compared to some of the more robust competitors, but won the event by about four inches.

The four relay heats and semi-finals were run during the evening; these included the 4 X 100 sprint and 4 X 400 events for both men and women. The United States teams were the fastest qualifiers in all four.

In the pole vault prior to the games there had been a very strong favourite to win the gold medal; the Russian, Sergei Bubka. He had broken the world record many times, and won the event in the world championships in 1993 and 1995. He had also won the

Olympic Gold medal in Seoul in 1988. Unfortunately, in the qualifying round earlier in the week, he had injured his Achilles tendon and was forced to withdraw from the competition.

In the final, 3 vaulters cleared a new Olympic record height of 5.92 metres – or 19ft 5 inches. In the pole vault and high jump, if a number of competitors all clear the same height, they apply a count back system where the judges look at the number of earlier failed attempts. The Frenchman, Jean Galfione cleared the height with his first attempt to win the gold medal. Tradenkov (Russia) and Tivontchik (Germany), although registering the same height, had missed at an earlier attempt. They had to settle for silver and bronze, due to the count-back.

The Americans had once reigned supreme in the pole vault, winning the gold medal in the first 16 Olympiads that had been held since 1896. These American winners included the 'vaulting vicar' Bob Richards, who won twice in 1952 and 1956. In 1960, the event was won by Don 'Tarzan' Bragg, who was said to have been promised the film role of *Tarzan* if he won the gold medal. He would walk around the athletes' village, practising the jungle cry that Johnny Weissmuller used in the earlier *Tarzan* films. He did win the event, but never appeared in a *Tarzan* film.

In front of the Atlanta crowd, the highest- placed American pole vaulter was Johnson in eighth place. The height he cleared was more than three feet higher than either Richards or Bragg had cleared in winning their gold medals, but then carbon fibres and pole technology have moved a long way in the past twenty to thirty years. There was very little flexibility in the old bamboo poles, whereas now the advanced technology of the carbon poles gives the vaulters a considerable advantage. Another factor is that, in the past, the vaulter landed in a sand-pit. Now they have a more comfortable foam cushion to break the fall.

I was standing beside the run-up from where I got a close-up view of the vaulter sprinting down the runway, jamming his pole into a box in the ground and then launching himself, feet-first to a height which was five feet higher than a double decker bus. He spun himself over the bar, then dropped down nearly 20 feet onto a foam- filled cushion. The courage of the competitors was amazing. From nearby, it looked absolutely terrifying.

The women's 10,000 metre race included several well-known distance runners; Deratu Tulu the current Olympic champion had won the event in Barcelona, and Wang Junxia had won the 5000 metres a few days before. As usual in a long distance track event, there was a large group of runners for the first half of the race and they started to drop off the pack from then onwards. Wang looked to have a good lead entering the final lap, but the Portuguese girl Fernanda Ribeiro kicked hard and won the race in a new Olympic record. The next six were either from Africa or the far-east.

The men's 3000 metres steeplechase is an event where the Kenyans reign supreme. Their stamina, speed and ability to suddenly change pace are well suited to a race where there are 28 hurdles and seven water jumps to be negotiated. Moses Kiptanui of Kenya was the clear favourite, as holder of the world record, and having won the world championship the last three times. Kenyans have an incredible record in this event and their three runners soon led the field. Joseph Keteer surprisingly won the gold medal with Moses Kiptanui about a second behind. Unexpectedly, the Italian Lambruschini beat the third Kenyan to prevent a one-nation podium medal ceremony. The American Marc Davis, who had raised the roof a few days earlier by storming home with an extravagant burning of energy to win his heat, didn't figure at all in the final. He just picked the wrong day to have his 15 minutes of glory.

Atlanta Olympic Games

Saturday 3rd August

When I arrived at the stadium it was almost empty, so I decided to have a good look around. I found two British volunteers sitting under the main scoreboard, using a lap-top computer. They said they had been sent to do some research into how the competitors threw the javelin. I did not have a chance to find out who sent them or what they learnt, as a local volunteer security guard stopped by to talk and, during the course of the conversation, he offered to lend me one of his company cars. As it was nearly the end of the games, I guessed that I would have little opportunity to use it, but it was very kind nevertheless. I asked him what the official procedure was for a volunteer security guard who found a suspicious object. His reply was, 'Leave it half an hour. If it doesn't go off then get a policeman to move it.'

Bruce's team had been allocated the section on the fourth level, which overlooked the high jump and the first take-over of the 4 X 100 relay. As you stepped out of the tunnel you faced a 60 foot drop that for a moment took your breath away. Some of the staff referred to this as the 'vomitory'. One woman spectator was so distressed by vertigo that her husband had to shield her eyes as she was directed to her seat. The heat was, as usual, intense and I was glad that on this day I had chosen to ignore the dress code and wear shorts instead of the heavy khaki drill trousers of the issued uniform.

The women's high jump and the men's javelin were taking place simultaneously. There was great British interest in the Javelin; there had been no gold medals in the athletics events so far and, when Steve Backley unleashed a fine throw in the first round to take the lead, I let out a roar of approval, as did many other British supporters dotted round the stadium. This caused some amusement from my fellow volunteers, as we were not allowed to show support for a competitor, for fear that it might offend other spectators who may be favouring another competitor. There had been so little for the British to cheer on the track earlier in the week, that this had hardly presented any problems. Here, at last, a British thrower had taken the lead. Sadly, in the next round, Jan Zelezny, the Czech defending champion unleashed an even greater throw to move ahead. That was how it finished. Steve Backley had done brilliantly to take the silver medal and had improved on the bronze medal he had won in Barcelona. I wondered what the javelin throwing researchers I had met earlier in the morning learnt from that.

The women's high jump was won by the Bulgarian Kostadinova, which was no surprise as she had dominated women's high jump for some time, winning the world championship a couple of times and also setting a world record. She had been to the last two Olympics as world-record holder, but failed to win the gold medal in either; winning the silver in Seuol, and coming fourth in Barcelona.

What was more interesting was watching the performance of the Greek silver medallist Niki Bakogianni, who cleared a height about 12 inches higher than she was. Other lankier female high jumpers seemed to tower over her. There were no British performers in this final, neither were there any Americans.

The men's 1500 metres, or the metric mile event has usually been regarded as the blue riband race. Britain had a fine record in the early Olympics, winning several medals of all hues in the event. More recently, there had been the purple patch of British performances with Coe, Ovett and Cram featuring in the medal ceremonies. In Atlanta, the balance of middle-distance power had definitely swung in favour of the African runners, although the Spanish runner Kacho was also in there with a shout. The Algerian Morceli was the world-record holder for 1500 metres and the mile; he was also world champion and had run a string of 50 odd races without defeat. However he had lost out in the previous Olympics in Barcelona due to poor tactics, when he was an overwhelming favourite. Neverthertheless, he was regarded as the favourite, although the Moroccan Hicham el Guerrouj, was also a strong contender. The Spanish runner Kacho was defending his Olympic title, and there was a group of formidable Kenyans.

In the final Morceli moved to the front of the pack with about a lap and a half to go, and started to open up the field, with el Guerrouj and Kacho trying to keep with him. Just before the bell for the final lap el Guerrouj was caught by someone's foot and crashed to the ground. Morceli went on to win a well-deserved gold medal, with defending champion Kacho in second place. A desolate el Guerrouj finished last. The story goes that he had a phone call from the King of Morrocco, who reassured him that he was still a national hero, and to carry on regardless. He went on to win double gold medals by winning the 1500 and 5000 metre races in Athens in 2004.

Just before the start of the 1500 metres, I was astonished to see a queue had formed in the concourse away from the seating area and out of sight of the track. There were nearly a hundred people standing in line to buy popcorn. I shouted to them that the 1500 metre race was about to start, but there was no interest; they clearly regarded the purchase of popcorn to be of greater importance than watching an Olympic 1500 metre final. They had probably paid two or three hundred dollars for the tickets, and one would have thought you could find plenty of places to queue for popcorn, without having to pay anything for a

143

ticket. The mindset of the American sports follower never ceases to astonish. Perhaps it's simply that there was no American competitor in this final.

Walking round the stadium later, I met Mary Peters, the lovely Irishwoman who had won the gold medal in the 1972 Munich Olympics for the women's pentathlon (later to become the heptathlon). She told me she was disgusted at the way the American supporters only focused on the performance of their own athletes, ignoring the other nations. She said she felt particularly badly about their reaction to Morceli and his victory ceremony.

The relays are really exciting events, and the Americans always have very good individuals, but when it comes to handing over the baton without dropping it, they sometimes come unstuck.

The 4 X 100 relay had been won by the US team 14 times in past Olympiads. Earlier in the week, Carl Lewis had won the long jump, taking an incredible ninth Olympic gold medal in his distinguished athletics career. Although he had not been involved in the US team relay training sessions, there were rumours that he had been campaigning for a place in the sprint relay team. No one had achieved 10 gold medals before in track and field events. For most of the week the media had been speculating about whether he would be selected to run in the 4 X 100 relay and make his tenth gold.

Other American sprinters expressed their views on the subject very strongly, particularly as they felt they had a justifiable place in the team, and that unlike

Lewis, they had attended the training sessions. No one wanted to relinquish their position in favour of Lewis. The coaches also had their views on team selection, and on the day when the team was announced it did not include the name of Carl Lewis.

The Canadian team were the current world champions, having taken the title in the world championships in Gothenburg the previous year. On the final leg for their team they had Donovan Bailey, who had taken the individual 100 metres gold a few days before. They were greatly incensed by the assumption that the US team were certainties to win, and that Carl Lewis only had to run to be assured of another gold medal.

There was some excitement at the start of the relay final as the Ghana team had picked an ineligible athlete for their team, and were disqualified. They refused to leave the track until the decision had been confirmed by the referee. All this meant that the start of the race was delayed by several minutes, much to the frustration of the other athletes all psyched up and raring to go.

When the race did get under way the lead-off Canadian sprinter was Robert Esmie. He had shaved his head showing the words 'Relay Blast Off'. He certainly did and made up ground on the American Drummond in the first leg. The Canadian baton changing was very slick and the American changes were not as good. By the final leg when Bruny Surin handed over to Donovan Bailey, Canada had a good lead of a couple of yards. He increased it by another

145

four yards storming away as befits a gold medallist. Bailey threw up his arms in celebration some yards before the finish, to win comfortably. Later he apologised to his team mates, as this action might have cost them the world record. Canada had won the gold medal convincingly from the American team. The home supporters were stunned into silence in our section of the stadium. An interesting snippit about the Canadian team; none of them were Canadian-born, all having been born around the Caribbean.

Fortunately for the home supporters, they had something to cheer about in the two women's relays when they won both races. Sadly in the shorter relay, the British team finished last.

For the final of the women's 1500 metres a couple of the favourites Boulmerka who was the title holder, and Sonia O'Sullivan had failed to qualify. Kelly Holmes of Great Britain gave us hope leading at the end of the third lap, but the Russian Svetlana Masterkova took the lead with 200 metres to go and went on to win. Sadly Kelly Holmes fell back and was well out of the medals. Her big days would come in Athens eight years later.

There were several medal ceremonies during the final afternoon, and most of them highly emotional. The home crowd had three gold medals to celebrate, however there were winners from several other nations on the rostrum including Kostadinova from Bulgaria in the women's high jump, Zelezny from Czech Republic, Morceli from Algeria, Niyongabo from Burundi in the 5000 metres, Masterkova of Russia in the women's 1500 metres and Canada in the sprint relay.

The final event of the day was the 4 X 400 relay, where there was just a chance of a British gold medal. It was the final track event of the Atlanta Olympic Games and, although there had been silver medals for Great Britain, we had not won a gold medal for track or field events. The American team was not their strongest as it did not include the mighty Michael Johnson nor Butch Reynolds, the 400 metre world record holder. The Americans were in front when the runners broke from the staggered lanes and it stayed that way throughout although the British team fought gamely. The Jamaican team had a faller, but he managed to get up and take third place. It was a two-horse race between USA and the British team with Roger Black on the final leg just failing to catch the leader. However the British team of Iwan Thomas, Jamie Baulch, Mark Richardson and Roger Black won a well -deserved silver medal.

After the final event, we had to sweep through our fourth floor area to clear out the spectators and ensure there was nothing left behind. Having completed that task, Bruce's team went down to the track side where many of the volunteers had gathered, mingling with a number of athletes. Our volunteer team stood on the winners' rostrum for a team photograph, and then we took a token jog around the track, just so we could say we had done it. The surface of the track close-up looked very much like a needle-cord carpet with a rubberised surface. It had been a thrilling and exciting final day on the track, but nevertheless very tiring. I was pleased to be able to get a lift home with Bruce, as the car ride was only forty minutes compared to nearly two hours by public transport. The marathon, the final event was due to start early in the morning and I was keen to be there for the finish.

Atlanta Olympic Games 1996

Sunday 4ᵗʰ August

The men's marathon started at 7.05 am to save the runners from the heat and humid conditions that are customary later in the day. I went to Buckhead, a few miles into the race, to watch the leaders run through. At this point there was a drinking station where water bottles were on the tables, and the runners snatched them as they ran by. There was a large group of at least 20 running together, and those nearest the table grabbed for a water bottle, took a swig, and passed them on to other runners in the group. Some simply poured the rest of the water over their heads, to help cool off. I caught the MARTA train to the stadium to watch the finish of the race.

In preparation for the closing ceremony later that evening, the grass in the centre of the track was completely covered in thick blue polythene sheeting. The track had a line of traffic cones for the runners to follow as they came into the stadium and headed towards the finishing tape. The stands alongside the finishing straight, and the back straight were about 50% filled, but around the bends they were empty.

It would have been nice if someone could have given information about who was nearing the stadium and identify who was on the track. From the point of view of the spectator, the finish of this Olympic Marathon was very poorly presented. I tried to get hold of a programme of some sort that would at least show the number that each athlete was wearing, but nothing so basic was available. There were no programmes to be had and very few details to help the spectators in the stadium. It was a shame as a lot of people present would have got more enjoyment from the event if someone could have told them what was going on. There was some brief information given over the public address system but it only related to the first five men to finish; there was no further information to identify the later finishers as they entered the stadium. Compared to the previous day when the finals were witnessed by a full stadium of over 80,000 spectators roaring their heads off when an American team was taking part, the finish of the marathon was witnessed by a just few thousand spectators, who applauded politely, rather like the crowd at a county cricket match.

I asked Steve Cram, who was in the commentary box how the British runner, Richard Nerurkar was doing; he said that he had been suffering from stomach problems. The finish of the race was very exciting in marathon terms, as the leading group of three runners entered the stadium within 30 yards of each other. The leader was a small South African, Josia Thugwane, closely followed by a Korean, Lee Bong Ju and in third place Eric Wainana of Kenya.

Bong Ju had overtaken Wainana as they entered the stadium, the race was that close. Thugwane won by three seconds, and the silver medallist was only five seconds ahead of the bronze. Without doubt, it was the tightest finish ever in the Olympic marathon. The fourth and fifth finishers had entered the stadium, before Thugwane had finished his final lap; the fifth man being Richard Nerurkar of Great Britain.

The marathon medal presentation took place later in the day, as part of the closing ceremony programme. Thugwane was little known, being ranked about 40th in the world before the race, and was the first black South African to win a medal. His medal ceremony was held in front of more than 80,000 spectators, and televised to two billion viewers round the world. If he was little known before the race, he certainly had exposure to the world audience now. "I've won it for my President", he said after the race. And mighty delighted was the President, Nelson Mandela.

There were some romantic stories about Thugwane. He had won several marathons in South Africa, but was little known outside his country. He was only 5ft 2inches and the smallest man in the field.

As a result of some of his races at home, he had won a few cash prizes and was therefore a marked man, by the South African criminal community. In March, some five months before the games, his car was hi-jacked by three armed thugs. As he was trying to escape from his car, he was shot in the chin, leaving a deep scar. He thought that his chances of running again were finished, but, after Atlanta he went on to other marathon successes, including finishing third the following year in the London Marathon. He also won the Great North Run Half-Marathon race, run in Gateshead.

Another interesting story concerned Wasigi, an entrant from Afghanistan, a country that had been devastated by war. A few weeks before the event, he had suffered an injury that prevented him from completing his training. After the start, he rapidly lost contact with the rest of the field, but kept going as a result of the support from those people alongside the route who liked to encourage the under-dog.

He eventually finished in 111th place. The man in front of him who finished in 110th place had come in one hour 20 minutes earlier. By the time he reached the stadium, the staff had already started to prepare for the closing ceremony that evening, and were covering the arena with large sheets of polythene. Fellow volunteers lined up alongside the track and cheered him all the way round, where someone had stretched a piece of polythene across the finishing line. His time was the slowest recorded in Olympic history,

4 hours 24 minutes and 17 seconds. This is the sort of stuff of Olympic legends.

There was still enough time, before I needed to report for the Closing Ceremony, to watch another event at the splendid Omni stadium. I had never watched the game of handball before, and although it is very popular in many countries in Europe, it is not played seriously in Britain. There was a bronze medal play-off between France and Spain. I was really impressed at the speed it was played, and the skills of the players in passing and catching the ball. When attempting to score, the players leapt in the air and hurled the ball overarm at the goal with great force. Spain won the bronze medal by beating France. Then there was the final between Croatia and Holland.

Now if ever a country deserved to win a gold medal for their handling of public relations, that country was Croatia. Attractive young Croatian girls were handing out free hats and scarves to the spectators. The hats were in the uniquely distinctive red and white check pattern, and the scarves had Croatia written in bold letters. Proudly wearing these freebies, I joined a group of neutrals who had adopted Croatia as their favourite team. Unfortunately, I could not watch the game to the end as it was time to report for duty, but I learnt later my favourites the Croatians, won the match and the gold medal.

Our team had been allocated the Presidential Box to manage. This involved showing the VIPs of the Olympic movement to their special places. The best six rows were allocated to the National Olympic

Committees and then four other areas where the seating was dependent on where the people stood in the Olympic administration pecking order. To determine this order, we were working with six special hosts, who were familiar with the Olympic hierarchy. Several of the volunteers were caught up in the popular craze of collecting pins. Each of the national teams had their own distinctive logos in the form of a lapel badge, which they handed out as a goodwill gesture. By the closing ceremony most of these had already been distributed. The volunteers displayed their badges by pinning them around their hats.

Several of the guests were taking photos of each other, so I offered to take their pictures with their own cameras for them, so they could include the whole group. This simple act seemed to delight many people to the extent that I was offered national pins without asking. It is remarkable how heavy 20-odd pins can be when displayed around a hat.

Spectators were expected to be in their seats by just after seven, although the programme was not scheduled to start until nine. From our position in front of the Presidential box, we had an excellent view. It started off with some music from the local youth Olympic band, who were really well rehearsed and gave an excellent performance. Then we enjoyed a cycle, roller blade and skateboard extravaganza, with a daredevil performance of youngsters swooping from one side to another on a steeply curved dish, flying into the air and performing a series of terrifying gymnastic activities on wheels. We then witnessed the most exciting medal ceremony of the whole games as Thugwane was awarded his gold medal. Of all the medal winners, he had undoubtedly the biggest audience both at the stadium and worldwide on television, in contrast to the small number of spectators at the finish of the race itself. He had the full band to play the South African national anthem; but after all he had needed to run 26 miles to win it.

As the next Olympiad was due to take place in Sydney in the year 2000, there was a 15 minute presentation by the Australian delegation. It started with a dozen or so Aboriginal dancers crouching on a circular stage with flames from a campfire in the background. They were accompanied by some digiridoo players; a ten-foot long tube-like instrument making a deep haunting hollow sound. They performed some unusual and highly original Aborigine dances.

Ten bike riders roared in with large inflated coloured kangaroos strapped to the their backs. The kangaroos dismounted and climbed on to the stage to join the dancing aborigines. Another team of female dancers dressed as cockatoos in an attractive yellow and white feathered outfit fluttered serenely around the Aborigines. A stream of blue Olympic flags was carried into the arena by the Australian life-saving team in their swimming costumes and caps, to circle the stage as an enormous replica of the Sydney Opera House made of white balloons rose up in the background - a very moving and artistic montage of the unique history and culture of Australia. Incidently, earlier in the week, Cathy Freeman an Australian Aborigine, had won the silver medal in the women's 400 metres.

There were the speeches, including one from the President of the International Olympic Committee, Juan Antonio Samaranch. In the days before the closing ceremony the press had been speculating whether he would give the Atlanta Games the accolade of the 'greatest ever Olympics'. He had declared at the end of the previous Olympics in Barcelona that those games had been 'the greatest ever'. He simply said "Well done Atlanta the 'most exceptional' Olympic Games." to the anger and despair of the locals. However he did award the gold Olympic Order medal to Billy Payne, the ACOG President and Chief Executive Officer. In the next games in Sydney, Samaranch resumed the habit by referring to them as the best Olympic Games ever.

There was a wonderful moment when six hundred Atlanta school-children aged from 6 – 12 came onto the stage singing 'The Power of the Dream', the song Celine Dion had sung at the opening ceremony a couple of weeks before. They were weaving around in single file forming intricate patterns, while carrying lit torches above their heads and swaying to the rhythm. One little ten-year old sang a solo part with amazing confidence and poise for one so young.

Cuban born, Gloria Estefan dressed in shimmering white was accompanied by the male choir dressed in black, ranged in a semi-circle behind her. Not only was there a contrast in the colour of their clothes but she was tiny compared to the choir backing her as she sang 'Reach' , an official song of the Games.

It was a very sad moment when the Olympic flame went out, but there was a spectacular fireworks display as a finale. As someone said, "The sky was blazing".

Finally, all the athletes went onto the centre of the arena informally. National teams mingled together in international fellowship, and jived. At this stage the volunteers moved onto the centre stage, taking photos of their team and friends made during the games

Sadly this most wonderful sporting festival was over; another four years before it would happen again. For every winner there were hundreds of others nursing their disappointments. There were athletes with injuries, or those who simply didn't perform at their best when it really mattered. It was great to see so many medals go to the smaller nations, and the totally unexpected victories like Rodal in the 800 metres or Thugwane in the marathon. There were moments of sheer brilliance with Michael Johnson smashing records and annihilating all opposition.

The next day about 250,000 sports followers flew out of the city of Atlanta.

Some thoughts about the Games.

The problem for any city promoting the Olympic Games is that the event is a complete 'one off'. The leaders have never done anything like it before and, having done it once, are unlikely to do anything on that scale ever again. Maybe every city wants to do it their way, and does not really want to listen to the hosts of earlier Olympiads. In the days leading up to the opening ceremony, you could feel the frantic rush to get the final details completed.

The MARTA, the railway system, was put under enormous strain, with hundreds of thousands of temporary passengers thrust upon it. The point of intersection where the two main lines crossed was the point at which the greatest stress was imposed. I can still recall the security men standing at the top and bottom of the escalators keeping people back to prevent them from overcrowding.

There were a number of athletes who complained bitterly that the transport was chaotic. Atlanta had called in many volunteer drivers from other states and many of them were totally unfamiliar with the area and, consequently competitors were arriving late for their events. Watching the opening ceremony with athletes charging down the ramp to catch up with the rest of their teams due to hold ups was an example of some of the transport problems.

The bomb explosion, where there were two fatalities and many others injured, threw an extra burden on the security staff. However from President Clinton downwards nothing was going to stop the games from continuing.

There was another fatality which had very little publicity. It occurred at the opening ceremony when the manager of the Polish National team collapsed and died. It was very sad that his unfortunate death received very little attention, and was not recognised in any way by the authorities. Perhaps just a mention in the closing speeches might have been possible.

There was supposed to be an Olympic mascot, a fantasy figure called Izzy, but it didn't seem to play much of a part in the games.

The information on each day's events was generally very poor. There was no sort of programme that you could pick up to show who was taking part in the heats, or finals at that session. It was also difficult to pick up detailed results sheets that would tell where those who failed to make the first three had finished. There seemed to be a conflict between the needs of the American public who were focused on American victories, and had little interest in the performances of competitors from other nations, and people from other nations who were interested in what was happening to their team, even if they were further down the field. The original Olympic ideal was once about taking part and not necessarily about winning, but then that was a 100 years ago.

After the games, part of the magnificent Centennial Olympic Stadium was demolished, reducing the seating capacity from 85,000 to 49,000. It became the home of the Atlanta Braves baseball team. The Atlanta-County stadium next door where the Olympic baseball games were played was demolished to become a parking lot for the baseball supporters. The Omni Coliseum where the volleyball matches took place was also demolished for a new arena to be built.

An interesting comment by a US Gymnast, Kerri Strug was printed in the *Sports Illustrated* magazine. She said, 'Having the Olympics in your home country is like a big national meet with some foreigners involved'. That seems to sum it up.

But for me to take part in the Centenary Olympic Games was a wonderful privilege. I made a lot of friends, I met some of the world's finest athletes, and enjoyed the friendship and warmth of the Southern States hospitality. If there was one moment for me that stood out from all the others it was the victory of Haile Gebrselassie in the men's 10,000 metres.

One event that I really regret not seeing was the fourth Olympic rowing gold medal won by Steve Redgrave, partnered by Matthew Pinsent in the coxless pairs, but then you can't expect to see everything.

What a fantastic three weeks. The role of the Olympic Volunteer is very demanding, and really quite exhausting but, as we were encouraged to do in the training manual I really believe that I made every minute count.

Without doubt the Olympic Games are the greatest show on Earth.,

©